Teaching Science in Elementary Schools

Books by the Same Author

Science Curriculum

Philosophy and Curriculum

Elementary Curriculum

Language Arts Curriculum

Improving School Administration

Teaching Mathematics in Elementary Schools

Teaching Social Studies in Elementary Schools

Teaching Science in Elementary Schools

Teaching Reading Successfully

Teaching Science Successfully

Teaching Mathematics Successfully

Teaching Social Studies Successfully

Teaching Language Arts Successfully

Teaching English Successfully

Modern Elementary School

Teaching Science in Elementary Schools

By

Dr. Marlow Ediger
M.S. Education, Ph.D.
Professor Emeritus in Education
Truman State University
Box 417, 201 W, 22nd St
North Newton KS 67117
United States of America

&

Dr. Digumarti Bhaskara Rao
M.Sc., M.A., M.A., M.Ed., Ph.D.
Reader & Research Director
R.V.R. College of Education
Srinivasa Nagar Colony
Guntur–522 006
(India)

DISCOVERY PUBLISHING HOUSE PVT. LTD.
NEW DELHI-110 002

First Published - 2003

Reprinted - 2019

ISBN: 978-81-7141-698-1

Teaching Science in Elementary Schools

Published by:

DISCOVERY PUBLISHING HOUSE PVT. LTD.
4383/4B, Ansari Road, Darya Ganj
New Delhi-110 002 (India)
Phone: +91-11-23279245; 23253475; 43596065
E-mail: discoverybooksindia@gmail.com
discoverypublishinghouse@gmail.com
web: www.discoverypublishinggroup.com

Printed at:
Infinity Imaging Systems
Delhi

To
A Great Educational Counsellor

Mr. Paturi Koteswara Rao
M.Sc.
Executive Director
Vignan Educational Institutions
Guntur-Visakhapatnam, Hyderabad

Preface

Teaching Science in Elementary Schools is written for pre-service and in-service education of elementary teachers. It integrates well in content with mathematics, social studies and languages. The contents will guide teachers to provide for individual differences so that each pupil may achieve as optimally as possible. As teachers need to keep up with the very latest in literature pertaining to teaching science in elementary schools, this book will help in teaching science effectively.

Dr. Marlow Ediger
Dr. Digumarti Bhaskara Rao

Contents

Contents

1

Teaching Science as Inquiry

Science teaching must reflect change within a curriculum that stresses assisting pupils to attain optimally. Objectives, learning opportunities, and appraisal procedures in science need to be relevant and updated to incorporate National and state standards. Units of instruction in science should stress inquiry, motivate pupils, and encourage high levels of interest. Educational philosophies and psychologies used in teaching-learning situations by the teacher must guide to pupils develop an inward desire to learn.

Philosophy of Science Teaching

The science teacher needs to have a wide repertoire or means of assisting pupils to achieve optimally. There are diverse educational philosophies for teachers to use that encourage optimal learner achievement.

First, a problem solving approach may be used. Inquiry learning is highly salient here. Ideally, pupils with teacher guidance need to identify a problem within the framework of an ongoing science unit of study. The problem must be clearly stated. Learners might then brain storm possible answers to the problem. Value judgements should not be made on responses given by pupils. The consequences or results of each brainstormed answer must be evaluated after the brainstorming session has been completed. A variety of manipulative, pictorial, and abstract materials should be used here. Science experiments may be at the heart of testing each response or hypothesis. Responses are then modified changed, or refuted as a result of the tests. John Dewey and other experimentalists emphasized problem solving strongly in their philosophy of experimentalism. Committee endeavours and cooperative learning are stressed in the problem solving science curriculum.

Experimentalists believe the science curriculum should be as closely related to the real world of society as possible. School and society are not separate but integrated entities. To emphasize problem solving, the science teacher must provide a learning environment that is stimulating and arouses pupil interests. Hopefully, the interests of learners will lead to problem identification. The goal of the science teacher is to have learners select relevant problems. The teacher becomes a resource person, guide, and helper, rather than one who lectures and presents content deductively to pupils. Thus learners need assistance in brain storming, locating reference sources, and attaining hypotheses as means of inquiry learning.

With pupils being heavily involved in selecting problems and strategies to solve each problem, a psychological curriculum is in evidence since each learner is heavily involved in sequencing or ordering his/her own experiences. The learner himself/herself tends to order experiences in a problem solving approach of teaching, according to educational psychologists. Pertaining to John Dewey's philosophy of experimentalism, Meyer (1949) wrote the following:

All this, of course, depends in no small way upon thinking. For Dewey, however, thinking becomes significant only when applied to life's situations. It is, he has said, "an instrumentality used by man in adjusting himself to the practical situations in life." Or to phrase it more simply, human beings think in order to live. Because to this stimulus, which has its basis in biology and sociology, it is impossible—it is absurd—to interpret life in a systematic and abstract way. Since, moreover, Dewey holds that life is in constant flux, it is impossible to solve problems with any degree of finality for the problems of tomorrow will be different from those of today.

As for the problem of knowledge, Dewey believes that knowledge is experience and that true experience is functional. What is this thing for? What is its use? Is a coal mine a physical deposit or does it have function? And if so, what is it? Such are the questions that help give meaning to one's experience; but such questions cannot be answered without antecedent action. Action must precede knowledge. Whatever knowledge we possess has resulted from our activities, our efforts to survive, to obtain food, shelter, and clothing. Only that which has been organised into our disposition so as to enable us to adapt our environment to our needs and to adapt our aims and desires to the situation in which we exist is really knowledge.

A second philosophy of education to stress is a subject centred science curriculum. Here, the science teacher must select and teach vital facts, concepts, and generalizations to pupils. Inquiry learning emphasizing critical and creative thinking, explanations, and vital discussions are methods of instruction used to teach learners. Intellectual development is a major objective of science instruction. Mind is real and needs challenging subject matter to encourage mental development. Cognitive objectives should be emphasized primarily. However, affective goals are also salient as they assist pupils to attain cognitive ends of science instruction. It is important to secure pupils interest in science, but each learner must also will to learn. Tasks in life are interesting as well as those that do not stress interest. Thus, the pupil must develop a will to achieve, attain, and develop well intellectually.

Subject centred approaches in teaching science emphasize the abstract instead of the concrete and semiconcrete facets of learning. The concrete (use of real objects, excursions, realia, and experiments), and the semiconcrete (illustrations, video-tapes, video-discs, computers with diverse capabilities, among other audio visual aids) should be used as learning opportunities to assist pupils to achieve the abstract. Thus objectives in teaching science need to stress the abstract in subject matter to be acquired as well as higher levels of cognition in ongoing units of study in science. The teacher largely determines which objectives and learning activities pupils are to pursue sequentially. Thus a logical science curriculum is being emphasized, according to educational psychologists. Ediger (1995) wrote:

Idealists are very academic and rigorous in the teaching of subject matter. They emphasize cognitive objectives much more so than affective (attitudinal) or psychomotor (use of muscles and eye-hand coordination) in teaching-learning situations. Meaning, understanding, and depth learning of subject matter are important to idealists. Vital subject matter, carefully selected, needs to be taught to students. The student in acquiring subject matter in ongoing lessons is to move from the finite (limited) to the Infinite being. Ideas are important to attain in an idealist's curriculum. The ideal is also salient to achieve in terms of moral standards and values.

The teacher emphasizing idealism as a philosophy of education stresses the selection of subject matter for student achievement which assists forming vital concepts and generalizations. Objectives of instruction need to reflect worthwhile concepts and generalizations. Depth teaching of specifics assisting students to form and develop universal ideas. The use of behaviourally stated objectives for instruction would be frowned upon by the idealist teacher. Content would become too fragmented with the realist's position of testing and measuring reflecting measurably stated objectives. Rather, the idealist in emphasizing an idea centred curriculum desires that students relate subject matter acquired so that intense learning transpires. Thus if students are studying causes of World War II, each cause would be studied thoroughly and not merely listed. Causes come in sequence and are complex to appraise. Viewing and analyzing each cause takes time. After analyzing, relating, or synthesizing ideas take time in order to emphasize intensity, not survey teaching. Students are to evaluated in progress as to how much vital subject matter has been acquired.

The use of the mind or intellect is salient for students to utilize in analyzing and synthesizing subject matter knowledge. Mental development is stressed as students learn, achieve, and develop.

Implications from idealism as a philosophy of education for the curriculum include the following:

1. intellectual, not attitudinal, nor psychomotor, goals come first in teaching-learning situations;
2. quality textbooks, workbooks, and selected audiovisual materials which aid in intellectual development should be used as learning activities to achieve stated goals for students;
3. evaluation techniques should stress appraisal of vital subject matter acquired by students;
4. depth teaching of subject matter is salient to guide learners to attain vital facts, concepts, and generalizations. Survey approaches are not acceptable;
5. that will of the student is needed to attain worthwhile subject matter. Interest of students, alone, is not adequate for students to achieve, attain, and develop well. Students must want to learn;
6. students need to achieve vital subject matter to prepare for the future life of an adult. Education is preparation for adult responsibilities, not present day situations in being a child;
7. learners need to develop form a finite (limited) being toward the Absolute or the Infinite (unlimited being). The Absolute may also be referred to as God;
8. a quality general education programme, consisting of vital content from major academic disciplines, is a must for all students.

A third philosophy of teaching emphasizes pupils being heavily involved in decision making in terms of choosing objectives, learning opportunities, as well as evaluation procedures. The science teacher needs to set up more stations with quality tasks than what any one pupil can complete. The pupil may then select sequential tasks to complete. Those tasks not having perceived purpose may be omitted by the learner. The teacher must choose relevant learning opportunities for pupils to select. Inquiry, problem solving, as well as critical and creative thinking tasks, are vital learning activities for pupils at each station. Careful consideration must be given to the worth of each station and task. The interests of pupils need to be cultivated in the science curriculum. The pupil is the chooser of which tasks to pursue and complete. The science teacher is a guide and stimulator but not a dispenser of information.

The attitudinal dimension is very important to develop within pupils when they select that which is vital to attain. Learners need to learn to make choices and decisions. Life itself consists of making choices within the framework of being openended and possessing freedom. In the science curriculum, pupils too need to make choices in which coercion is kept to a minimum. A decision making philosophy stress the learner being responsible for choices and completions made. Decision making is a skill and an attitude that pupils should learn due to its tremendous value presently and in the future for pupils.

With pupils being heavily involved in choosing sequential tasks to complete, a psychological curriculum is them in evidence due to pupils sequencing their very own activities in the science curriculum.

Pertaining to existentialism and pupil choices in the curriculum, Ozman and Craver (1990) wrote:

It is interesting that most existentialists and phenomenological philosophers have had lengthy and rigorous educations... Most of them taught at one time or another, usually in a university setting. They have been primarily concerned with the humanities and have written exclusively in the genre. Through the humanities the existentialists have tried to awaken modern individuals to the dangers of being swallowed by the megalopolis and runaway technology. This seems to have taken place because the humanities contain greater potential for introspection and the development of self-meaning than other studies.

The humanities loom large in an existentialists curriculum because they deal with the essential aspects of human existence such as the happy, the absurdities as well as meaning. In short, existentialists want to see humankind in its totality—the perverted well as the exalted, the mundane as well as the glorious, the despairing as well as the hopeful, and they feel that the humanities and the arts do this better than the sciences. Existentialists, however do not have any definite rules about what should comprise the curriculum. They believe that the student-in-situation making a choice should be the deciding factor.

Although existential phenomenologists have been interested in understanding the lived experience of the learner than in the specific content to be learned, some of them have given attention to curriculum organisation and content. The tendency, however, is to view curriculum from the standpoint of the learner rather than as a collection of discrete subject matter.

A fourth philosophy of education for science teachers to follow is a criterion referenced (CRT) procedure of instruction. Here the teacher needs to write measurably stated objectives for pupil attainment. These objectives are always written prior to teaching pupils. Each objective is written in as precise a manner as possible. Ideally there is no leeway in interpreting what will be taught when examining any one measurably stated objective. The science teacher can measure after instruction if a learner has or has not achieved a measurably stated objective. The CRT measures against the measurably stated objectives to ascertain pupil achievement.

Science teachers may even announce to pupils what they are to learn as a result of instruction. Learners then might possess security in terms of what they are expected to achieve as a result of teaching and learning. Learning activities selected by the teacher to assist pupils to achieve must be aligned with the measurably stated objectives. These activities must be selected on the basis of guiding each pupil to achieve objectives. A logical curriculum is in evidence if the teacher chooses sequential objectives for pupil attainment as well as learning opportunities that are sequentially arranged so that pupils can experience success in learning.

Since teachers determine the sequence of objectives and learning opportunities for pupils to pursue, a definite logical curriculum is being stressed by science teachers. The teacher then attempts to arrange the order of objectives and activities to guide optimal pupil achievement. Pertaining to realism, Bowyer (1970) wrote the following:

> We have noted that there are different forms of naturalism and of idealism. The same is true of realism, which makes it difficult to define the realist point of view. One element that the various forms of realism do have in common is a rejection of the idealist theory of knowledge that the various qualities of experience depend upon a knower for their existence. Realists believe the universe is composed of real entities that exist in themselves. These entities can be known, and their existence is not dependent upon a knower or perceiver. Although realists can agree on this point, they do not all agree when they attempt to build a metaphysical system. Here, their views range from pluralism to dualism to monism.
>
> The realist epistemological views include epistemological monism where it is held that objects are presented in consciousness, and epistemological dualism where objects are thought to be represented. The monist defines mind as a relation between the organism and an object, while the dualists identify mind more closely with the organisms. Realists do have a tendency to view the world as the mechanism described by the physical sciences, and they generally believe in determinism, in orderliness in the universe, and the objectivity of science. The unifying thesis of realism is that knowledge is

thought to have a universal character and comes to man through his sensory capacity. The realists have a confidence in their assertions about reality and value which is most discerning to pragmatists.

Recent Psychologies of Learning

B.F. Skinner (1904-1990) was very instrumental in emphasizing S-R. theory of instruction. With S-R theory in teaching science. Skinner advocated programmed learning for pupils. Programmed learning can take place either in textbook or computer/software form. Here, pupils move forward very slowly from the simple to that which is gradually more complex. Pupils then respond to a logical sequence developed by the programmer. Thus the pupil reads a small amount of content, responds to a completion item, and checks his/her response with that provided by the programmer. If the pupil responded correctly, he/she moves on to the next sequential item. If the learner responded incorrectly, he/she tries a different response. If correct, the learner also moves on to the next sequential item. The sequence is the same each time with read, respond, and check. If the learner is correct, he/she is rewarded and reinforced for giving the correct answer to the completion item as provided by the programmer. Skinner believes that a programmer can always put in another item should the pupil taking the programme in the pilot study miss out in a sequential item. A quality programme should make for a ninety per cent correct pupil response per item for each in the pilot study. The pilot study involves conducting experiments to find out where weaknesses lie in the programme. If to many learners, miss an item, perhaps an additional step needs to be put in where these pupils responded incorrectly. Poorly written items are taken out or modified so that responses can be made based on clarity within that step of learning. I have observed selected well written programmes in science units of study which reflect the thinking of B.F. Skinner. Pertaining to programmed learning, Harris and Sipay (1985) wrote the following:

Programmed materials are designed so that the user (1) encounters a series of small steps on which success is very likely (2) is involved in the learning process through actively responding (3) receives immediate feedback as to the correctness of each response. In theory, programmed material should greatly facilitate individualized instruction because they allow each student to work almost independently with material suitable for his or her needs, proceeding at a pace commensurate with ability and interest.

Ediger (1997) wrote the following pertaining to programmed instruction:

The programmer decides upon the objectives for each programme. Also, the sequential activities and appraisal procedures are determined by the programmer. There is basically no input from pupils or from teachers in terms of objectives, learning activities, and evaluation procedures when utilizing programmed materials.

Advantages given for using programmed learning include the following:

1. each learner may pace his/her own optimal speed of learning. No two pupils need to be at the same or similar level of achievement;
2. learners know immediately if they are right or wrong in responses made;
3. rarely do learners make mistakes in quality programmed materials. The error rate is five to ten per cent in field tested programmes;
4. reinforcement is possible in field tested programmed items. Thus an involved learner might experience rather continual progress;
5. sequential progress is made in small steps rather than covering content in terms of a large scope at a time.

Disadvantages given in emphasizing programmed learning include:

1. programmed learning may not harmonize with learning styles of selected pupils;
2. step by step learning—read, respond, and check—does not harmonize with expectations of life in society. Life in society is not programmed;
3. programmed materials tend to deemphasize the utilization of the concrete (reality), and semi-concrete (pictorial form) materials;
4. selected pupils may not perceive interest and purpose in the programmer choosing objectives, learning activities, and evaluation procedures;
5. small sequential steps in learning may be too finite or limited to meet personal needs of gifted and talented learners.

The influence of programmed learning and the thinking of B.F. Skinner has had wide influence in educational thought. There still are programmed books available on many topics in book form as well as in computer packages. Perhaps, the strongest influence of Dr. Skinner is in the use of behaviourally stated objectives in teaching. These objectives are very precise and are written prior to instruction. A pupil as a result of instruction either does or does not achieve any single objective. Thus, it is possible to measure if a pupil has been successful in goal attainment. Learning activities selected by the teacher align with the stated objectives. The evaluation procedures also are aligned with the measurably stated objectives. Objective results from pupils are in evidence from instruction, regardless of who does the evaluating. Relating B.F. Skinner's thinking and that of the behaviourally stated objectives movement, the following writing will assist in clarifying the two (Morris and Pai, 1976):

As Skinner pointed out several times, the most important task of the teacher is to arrange the conditions under which desired learning can occur. Considering the fact that teachers are expected to bring about changes in extremely complex behaviour, they shouɪd be specialists in human behaviour.

Effective and efficient manipulation of the multitude of variables affecting children's intellectual and social behaviours cannot be accomplished by trial and error alone, nor should such work be based solely on the personal experiences of the teacher,since this covers only a limited range of circumstances. Consequently a scientific study of human behaviour is vital in the improvement of teaching, because it provides us with accurate and reliable knowledge about learning and leads us to the development of new instructional materials, methods, and techniques. Similarly, an empirical analysis of the teaching process is essential, for it clarifies the teacher's responsibility through a series of small and progressive approximations, thus facilitating a more effective evaluation.

The measurably stated objectives movement, also called behaviourism as a psychology of learning, emphasizes a rather closed system of instruction. The objectives are predetermined and may be announced to pupils for each end to be stressed, as the need progresses, the learning activities and the evaluation techniques harmonize or align. Many educators believe that this alignment optimalize learner achievement in teaching and learning situations.

With this close alignment, little room is left for pupils to raise questions that they deem to be relevant and vital.

Humanism in the Science Curriculum

Toward the other end of the continuum, humanism, as a psychology of learning stresses heavy pupil involvement in selecting objectives, learning opportunities, and appraisal procedures, the pupil here is the focal point of instruction. Learners are to involve in sequencing their own experiences; this emphasizes a psychological science curriculum whereas the behaviourally stated objectives psychology advocated a logical sequence for pupils whereby the teacher orders objectives for pupil attainment. Pertaining to humanism and existentialism. Ediger (1996) wrote:

Existentialists believe that one exists and then purposes need to be found or developed. The individual self then determines his/her own goals in life. There are no absolutes or guidelines in life to choose what is right and what is good. Each person must select and make decisions. To avoid making decisions is to lack being human. The choice then is to go along with the crowd. However, to be human involves making decisions.

The only broad criterion for existentialists to follow in choosing is to make moral decisions in a complete atmosphere of freedom. Others should definitely not decide one's destiny. One did not ask to be born and yet each person must make authentic decisions.

Moral decisions are difficult to make. An environment of awe exists in making authentic decisions.

Which objectives, learning activities, and evaluation procedures should be inherent in an existentialists curriculum? Existentialists believe in each person choosing objectives. In the schools setting, the goals may be selected by learners with teacher guidance within the framework of an open-ended curriculum. The teacher needs to select ends, means, and evaluation procedures which stress the importance of pupils becoming increasingly responsible for personal freedom. The teacher should definitely not be a policeman. Rather, teachers realize their role as providing for an open environment in order that the learner may select sequential experiences...

Each decision made in life involves personal decisions in reaching a goal or goals... Each person makes or breaks himself or herself. No other person or being is responsible for consequences of decisions made. Blaming others for what happened in life in meaningless, according to existentialists. Each person needs to learn to accept responsibilities for thoughts, deeds, and actions.

The humanist or existentialists science curriculum may be implemented in several ways. One approach is to use learning centres in the school/classroom setting. One of the authors have observed the following learning centres pertaining to the science unit. "The Changing Surface of the Earth," from which pupils may select sequential tasks to complete:

1. a reading centre;
2. an art centre;
3. a drama centre;
4. a writing centre;
5. an audio-visual centre;
6. a computer and software centre;
7. a music centre;
8. a model making centre;
9. a problem solving centre;
10. an experiment centre.

Each pupil in a classroom may select which centre and which task to work on. There are more tasks at each centre than what any one child can complete. Learners may then chose what to work on and what to omit in a humanistic science curriculum. The individual pupil determines sequence or order of which tasks to pursue and which to omit. Purpose for learning then reside within the pupil. Examples of which materials will be at a learning centre and the kinds of tasks or learning activities that will be in evidence may be illustrated with the first centre mentioned above—a reading centre. Here, a variety of library books on the unit title and on diverse reading levels need to be in evidence. A pupil chooses a book to read and may complete as many of the following tasks at this centre as individual purpose dictates:

1. write a summary covering content read;
2. make a model of inherent subject matter read, such as a model volcano;
3. draw a picture of folding and faulting;
4. write an additional page for the library book read;
5. identify a problem dealing with changes on the earth's surface and use various reference sources to locate information for solving the problem.

Pupils individually make choices sequentially as to what to learn and the means of learning. Tasks can relate to choosing to work by the self or with others. If too many work at one centre, the teacher may make a rule as to the optimal number of pupils that may work at any one centre. The science teacher here is a guide or motivator of pupils to stay on task and complete satisfactorily what has been selected as learning activities. The pupil may even plan with the teacher what to work on if greater purpose is perceived in working on something else than what is at any of the centres.

Humanists advocate that pupils reveal authentic behaviour, not facades, to be authentic, the pupil needs to reveal more of the real self. Trust in communicating with others is important. Humans have tremendous worth and value. Being authentic and trusting others in a positive relationship is relevant to humanists.

Many studies currently made stress the importance of multiple intelligences. Sternberg (1997) emphasizes that in a Yale University study, intelligence has analytical, creative, and practical aspects. He presents the following model for science in four categories:

Memory— name the four types of bacteria.

Analysis— analyze the means the immune system uses to fight bacterial infections.

Creativity— suggest ways to cope with the increasing immunity bacteria are showing to antibiotic drugs.

Practicality— suggest three steps that individuals might take to reduce the likelihood of bacterial infection.

In any lesson and unit of study, the science teacher may emphasize these four categories of instruction. Pupils need to achieve at higher levels of cognition than the memory level. Learners will then reveal in different ways what has been learned in the analysis, creativity, and practicality levels. Intelligence then is not a single score nor a single way of indicating what has been learned. Sternberg (1997) goes on to say:

By exposing students to instruction emphasizing each type of ability, we enable them to capitalize on their strengths while developing and improving new skills. This approach is also important because students need to learn that the world cannot always provide them with activities that suit their preferences. At the same time, if students are never presented with activities that suit them, they will never experience a sense of success and accomplishment. As a result, they may tune out and never achieve their full potential...

Success in today's job market often requires creativity, flexibility, and a readiness to see things in new ways. Furthermore, students who graduate with A's but cannot apply what they have learned may find themselves failing on the job.

Creativity, in particular, has become even more important over time, just as other abilities have become less valuable. For example, with the advent of computers and calculators, both penmanship and arithmetic skills have diminished in importance, some standardized ability tests, such as the SAT, even allow students to use calculators. With the increasing availability of massive, rapid data retrieval systems, the ability to memorize information will become even less important...

This is not to say that that memory and analytical abilities are not important. Students need to learn and remember the core content of the curriculum, and they need to be able to analyze—to think critically about—the material. But the importance of these abilities should not be allowed to obfuscate what else is important.

In a pluralistic society, we cannot afford to have a monolithic conception of intelligence and schooling, it's simply a waste of talent. And as I unexpectedly found in my study, it's no random waste. The more we teach and assess students based on a broader set of abilities, the more racially, ethnically, and socioeconomically diverse our achievers will be. We can easily change our closed system—and we should. We must take a more balanced approach to education to reach all of our students.

Stenberg believes strongly that pupils individually are not permitted to indicate what has been learned in diverse ways. It is true that pupils so often are asked to show achievement through testing, generally through pupils taking multiple choice tests. Thus verbal approaches are used to ascertain what pupils individually have learned. This is limiting in that there are many other means of revealing achievement. Dr. Howard Gardner (1995) has determined there are at least seven intelligences, according to his research; these are verbal-linguistic, interpersonal, intrapersonal, musical, spatial, bodily-kinesthetic, and logical mathematics. Pupils may show similar strengths, but not necessarily in the same ways or to the same extent over time. With multiple intelligences, pupils learn in diverse ways and are interested in different subject matter in the academic arena. Learners then reveal their strengths and weaknesses in what has been learned in a variety of ways, not one way only such as in verbal testing using multiple choice items. Thus, the pupil who is strong in the verbal arena will reveal differently what has been learned as compared to the one endowed with musical intelligence. Too frequently, the emphasis has been upon verbal approaches to assessing pupils achievement and yet there are numerous other ways to indicate intelligence, as Dr. Gardner has indicated in multiple intelligences theory. Hatch (1997) wrote:

Such a view of intelligence is reflected in programmes and practices that seek to determine which areas young children show the greatest strengths. Children who do well on tasks in a particular area—storytelling or reporting, athletics or dance, drawing or building—are broadly labelled as having strengths in linguistics, bodily-kinesthetic, or spatial realms, respectively.

Such an approach, however, implies that children have a reservoir of talent in a variety of activities, shown consistently over a period of time. It suggests that there are more intelligences, but does not necessarily call into question assumptions about the nature, display, and development of intelligence.

In Summary

Science teachers need to develop a philosophy and psychology of instruction that optimalize learner attainment. Pupils differ from each other in many ways including methods and procedures of acquiring relevant facts, concepts, and generalizations. A careful study and implementation of a worthwhile philosophy and psychology of learning might well assist each pupil to learn as much as possible.

To stress science as inquiry in harmony with National Standards, the writers emphasize what they believe to be best from each school of thought discussed above. These are:

1. a problem solving science curriculum in which pupils with teacher guidance identify and solve relevant lifelike problems;
2. a subject centred science curriculum emphasizing pupils attaining higher levels of cognition in achieving salient facts, concepts, and generalizations;
3. pupil selection from among alternatives of tasks perceived to be purposeful. Tasks at different stations should reflect science as inquiry;
4. measurably stated objectives which reflect National Standards in a predetermined science curriculum. Precise objectives are then selected prior to instruction for learner attainment. A carefully designed science curriculum may then be in evidence. The content obtained should be inherent in science as inquiry teaching and learning.

Pertaining to the psychology of learning in science, pupils should achieve quality sequence. Interest, purpose, and meaning are important concepts to stress in teaching science in ongoing lesson plans and units of study.

With multiple intelligences theory, pupils do learn in different ways and through diverse methods of instruction. Learners individually do possess their favourite means of learning and achieving. There are numerous methods of revealing what has been learned.

The science teacher then needs to have pupils participate in a variety of learning opportunities and have them indicate achievement using diverse procedures to provide for different learning styles possessed. The following learning opportunities are available for pupils in the science curriculum:

1. hands on approaches in learning;
2. experiments and demonstrations;
3. field trips and excursions;
4. problems solving experiences;
5. reading from basal texts, library books, and science encyclopaedias;
6. viewing video tapes, video disks, films, and filmstrips;
7. discussing, interviewing, dramatizing, and pantomiming;
8. writing poems, plays, outlines, summaries, diary entries, log entries, journal entries, and stories;
9. making dioramas, collages, bulletin board display, murals, models, and equipment for science experiments;
10. using technology such as computer packages, the word processor, internet and world wide web, and calculators.

REFERENCES

Bowyer, Carlton (1970). *Philosophical Perspectives for Education*. Glenview, Illinois: Scott, Foresman and Company, Page 17.

Ediger, Marlow (1995). *Philosophy in Curriculum Development*. Kirksville, Missouri: Simpson Publishing Company, Pages 22 and 23.

Ediger, Marlow (1997). *The Modern Elementary School*. Kirksville, Missouri: Simpson Publishing Company, Pages 110 and 111.

Ediger, Marlow (1996). *Essays in School Administration*. Kirksville, Missouri: Simpson Publishing Company. Pages 58 and 59.

Ediger, Marlow and Digumarti Bhaskara Rao (2003). *Philosophy and Curriculum*. New Delhi, India: Discovery Publishing House.

Gardner, Howard (1995). "Reflections on Multiple Intelligences:

Myths and Messages," *Phi Delta Kappan* 77, 3:200-203, 206-209.

Harris, Albert J., and Edward R. Sipay (1985). *How to Increase Reading Ability*. White Plains, New York: Longman, Page 71.

Hatch, Thomas (1997). "Getting Specific About Multiple Intelligences," *Educational Leadership*, 54, 6: 26.

Meyer, Adolph (1949). *The Development of Education in the Twentieth Century* Englewood Cliffs. New Jersey: Prentice-Hall, Inc., Pages 42-43.

Morris, Van Cleve, and Young Pai (1976). *Philosophy and the American School*. Boston: Houghton Mifflin Company, Page 340.

Ozman, Howard A., and Samuel M. Craver (1990). *Philosophical Foundations of Education*. Columbus, Ohio: Merrill Publishing Company, Pages, 257.

Sternberg, Robert J. (1997), "What Does It Mean to be Smart? *Educational Leadership*, 22-24.

2

Current Events in Science

Pupils desire to experience relevant content in science. The content then needs to be based on the interests and needs of learners. Who determines these interests and needs? The pupil should be in the best position to determine what is relevant. He/she decides what is useful and has application values. One way of approaching the problem of ascertaining relevancy is for the teacher to develop and provide learning stations for pupils whereby each pupil may select that task or learning activity which as the greatest value when engaging in sequential learning experiences. There should be enough tasks at the different stations so that learners may omit what does not possess perceived relevancy and yet have plenty of work to do.

A second approach in teaching is to use teacher—pupil planning within the framework of a thematic unit of study. The science teacher then plans with the pupils that which the latter wishes to learn. There may be large class, collaborative experiences within committees, as well as individual study activities. Thus, the teacher assists pupils to determine objectives, learning opportunities, and evaluation procedures that possess relevancy.

A third approach in deciding upon relevant topics for pupils to pursue in the science curriculum is for teachers, principals, and supervisors to study, analyze, and accept thematic units of study involving consensus thinking. This might well incorporate state mandated objectives as well as the National Science Teachers Association standards for learners to achieve in the science curriculum. Clearly written objectives, quality learning opportunities for pupils to attain the objectives, as well as valid/reliable evaluation procedures to ascertain if pupils have attained the stated objectives of instruction must then be in the offing.

We would like to suggest a fourth approach which emphasizes a current events procedure. Pupils may hear news items in the home setting pertaining to what is happening currently in the natural environment. Current events indicate that the happening is occurring at the present time and is of concern to many people.

Current Events in Science

What is transpiring presently has many natural phenomena for pupil study. At this writing, there are devastating floods in Oregon and to some extent in Washington. Annual floods occur in different areas around the world. People lose homes, lives, cars, furniture, and other property in flood waters. Floods carry much energy with the damage that these high waters can do. Learners then find floods to be a natural phenomenon that occur frequently. It is a very worthy topic and theme to study if human being wish to do something to deter the devastating happenings that result from floods. Newspapers, TV and radio news reports, news magazines, video tapes, multiple series basal texts, science encyclopaedias, computer packages, internet, and videodisks, among other materials of instruction, might well provide appropriate content for pupils to use in problem solving such as:

1. identifying and answering questions involving "What causes floods to occur?";
2. securing information in problem solving activities;
3. developing a hypothesis or tentative answer to the question/problem;

4. testing the hypothesis when reading and acquiring information to approve or refute the hypothesis;
5. revising the hypothesis if necessary as a result of the test.

When studying about floods, pupils should also learn what human beings do to try to alleviate the suffering that occurs from these problematic situations. Social studies here becomes a part of the science curriculum. An integrated, interdisciplinary curriculum results. Pupils then need to learn about the work of the Red Cross, relief organisations which provide clean up crews with no costs involved, as well as state, country, and federal efforts working toward remedying problems involving flooding.

A second natural disaster which occurred two weeks ago, at this writing, was freezing rain in the southern eastern states of the US. North Carolina, an entire state, dismissed schools and business work days for one day due to electric wires being down, roads being slick and unsafe, and tree limbs blocking areas for driving. Freezing rain which damages electrical lines and makes roads slick occurs when the temperature reading goes below thirty-two degrees Fahrenheit and moisture falls in the form of rain. The costs of freezing rain might well run into the billions of dollars and cause many accidents and deaths from slick road surfaces.

Pupils need to learn about causes for freezing rain. They should learn about hazards that occur and why. Safety should be discussed and taught when freezing rain comes about. Goals of instruction pertaining to the phenomenon of freezing rain should be relevant and important for pupils. Learners need to have opportunities to work individually and collaboratively in problems identified pertaining to learning about freezing rain. A variety of materials need to be used by pupils in finding answers to problems. Depth teaching should be in emphasis. Intensive learning about freezing rain and its consequences should be an end result.

Sequence in learning may follow a logical approach whereby the science teacher sequences or orders the learning opportunities for pupils. At other times a psychological sequence may be followed in that learners with teacher guidance may order experiences and activities. Methods of teaching should involve induction, deduction, guided instruction by the teacher, as well as pupils with teacher guidance planning the ongoing lessons and units of study pertaining to natural disasters.

Three years ago at this writing, California had a series of earthquakes with its accompanying after shocks, China, Japan, Russia, the Ukraine, and Iran, among other nations on the planet earth, experience rather frequent problems pertaining to earthquakes as a natural phenomena. Property and road damage can be high indeed depending upon the severity of the quake as measured by the Richter scale. Destruction to buildings might well depend, in part, upon how these were built and which materials were used, pertaining to earthquakes online, Butler, et. al. (1996) wrote:

Earthquakes provide a perfect interdisciplinary teaching opportunity to involve students in highly motivational real-world experiences. Access to information regarding earthquakes is available from several sources on the internet, but the primary source is the National Earthquake Information Service (NEIS) in Golden, Colorado. This service is provided by the US Geological Survey... The site gives near-real-time international information on earthquakes. For each earthquake, the following data are provided: the time in Universal Time, the latitude and longitude of the epicentre, the depth in kilometres to the focus, the magnitude, and the general location.

To implement the earthquake project, access to a computer with a modem, a printer, and an Internet account is necessary. In addition to the hardware, the real ingredient necessary for a successful project is a group of motivated teachers. In our district this mix of material and personnel was located at Canton Middle School, Las Vegas, Nevada. The lead teacher was a science teacher, who has supported by a geography teacher and a mathematics teacher.

The science teacher, who has the Internet connection in the classroom, introduced students to the internet. On the first day of the programme, one student from each class period was trained to use the computer and modem to access NEI's earthquake reporting site. The following day, students who had been trained each trained another student... In the weeks that followed, each student became a trainee and a trainer in turn...

A large Mercator projection map of the Earth was posted on a bulletin board in the science classroom. Each day as information was gathered, groups of students located the epicentre of each earthquake reported on the map using pushpins color coded according to earthquake magnitude...

Objectives for instruction should be developed cooperatively by teachers with supervisor assistance. Careful evaluation of each objective is a must. The learning activities for pupils to attain vital objectives need to be conducive to helping pupils attain as optimally as possible. Pupil interests, needs, purposes, and attitudes need proper provision so that quality achievement in these areas are in evidence. Appraisal procedures to determine pupil attainment of goals need to be varied so that each facet of achievement is evaluated. Teacher developed, norm referenced, as well as criterion referenced tests may be used to ascertain pupil achievement of vital objectives. Anecdotal records, journal writing, teacher observation, pupil self evaluation, learner products of instruction, class participation, videotapes, and snapshots of learner achievement need to be in the offing to reveal and indicate the quality of pupil achievement. Thus a variety of procedures should be used to determine how much pupils have learned pertaining to natural disasters on the planet earth.

Four years ago, several of the plains states were hit by tornadoes. One tornado in central Kansas uprooted evergreen trees ten feet tall and eleven inches in diameter. A half mile away, a newly built sturdy brick house had just been completed as a dream house for a retired couple. This durable structure was completely demolished by the 150 miles per hour winds in the tornado. Houses in the path of the tornado that remained standing were damaged to the point where they were later torn down. The path of the tornado could be followed easily in terms of where devastating destruction had occurred. Farm houses and barns, directly adjacent, were unharmed. There is tremendous energy in the force of tornadoes.

Pupils with teacher guidance then need to

1. identify relevant problems areas to solve;
2. choose subject matter content which supplies needed answers;
3. select from the acquired subject matter that which provides tentative answers to the question;
4. check the accuracy of the answer(s) through additional study;
5. notice additional problem areas pertaining to tornadoes that would be relevant to solve.

Cyclones and hurricanes may be incorporated into the study of tornadoes. Pupils also need to view each natural disaster in terms of what human beings can do to minimize its destructive forces as well as what can be done to alleviate human suffering.

Lightning strikes buildings and kills human beings, perhaps not to the extent that the previously discussed natural disasters do. A barn or shed filled with hay bales and farm implements may be struck by a bolt of lightning causing the property to be completely destroyed. Millions of dollars worth of labour and property burn ferociously, even with fire departments out in full force in rural areas. It is costly to remove the remains such as bulldozers dozing the concrete floors and slabs, from the destroyed buildings, to be hauled away by trucks. Trash from the burning property needs to be disposed of using bulldozers to load the contents onto trucks. Thus the hauling away of trash after lighting has hit a building is labour intensive and expensive.

The science teacher needs to identify key structural ideas that pupils should achieve pertaining to lightning and its affects on people and the environment. Forests, among other areas, can be damaged much due to being hit by lightning. This is easy to observe when travelling through any wooded area, small or large.

Drouth, as another natural disaster, keeps farm crops from producing or makes water scarce for livestock and other rural needs. Farmers and ranchers can be bankrupted when drouth hits an area. Livestock has to be sold cheaply since no one can afford to care for these animals when feed costs become very high due to scarcity and greed. It has an opposite affect as compared to farm crops being destroyed due to floods or excessive rain. Drouth has as a consequence a lack of water in cities for watering the lawn or washing the car, luxuries perhaps.

When farm land has drought and strong winds are in evidence, erosion of soil can well be an end result. Erosion of top soil is difficult to restore. The farmer can minimize erosion through terracing, strip cropping, as well as growing grass and trees on farm land. All of these measures to control soil erosion are costly and tend to bring in minimal farm income. For example, quality hay, baled from excellent grassland, will not provide the income to farmers as compared to cultivated land where wheat, corn and soybeans are grown. Generally an inch of eroded top soil takes 100 to 500 years to rejuvenate.

Pertaining to drouth as a natural disaster, we recommend the following questions and issues for pupils to pursue using a variety of learning opportunities:

1. How can a balanced be established between farmers making a living from farming as compared to using proper methods of preventing soil erosion?

2. Should there be federal and state government payments to farmers to prevent soil erosion, wetlands protection, as well as other means of protecting soil in the natural environment?
3. How can the natural environment best be protected, especially in the area of soil protection?

The use of pesticides and herbicides has become increasingly common to control harmful insects and weeds. If pesticides were not used, the chances are that our food supply would be greatly reduced due to sharing more and more of it with insects and other pests. Apple damage from moths can indeed be extensive. The corn borer, as well as smut, can greatly minimize yields in corn production. The Colorado potato beetle, in larva stage, can strip an otherwise good crop of potatoes in a matter of two to three days. A hoard of grasshoppers can cause extensive damage, in a few days, to growing soybean plants. The reasons for using pesticides is quite obvious. Farmers may experience huge financial losses from insects and other pests in a short time of hours or a few days.

Weeds also can do much damage to farm crops in a few days. Cockleburs, for example, can crowd out soybean plants, in a week, from securing needed moisture and sunlight Herbicides when used may completely destroy all cockleburs in a matter of hours. Gardeners realize that foxtail weeds might well take all the moisture away from growing garden crops. How to minimize weed damage in the growing of farm crops as well as to prevent damage to ornamental plants can indeed be a problem. Pesticides and herbicides can control insect population and weed growth. Increasingly, there are more resistant strains of insects and weeds to pesticides and herbicides. When DDT first came out in 1944, there was much optimism about its future in controlling flies, mosquitoes, and other pests that hinder livestock production. DDT initially was very successful in curbing flies, insects, and other pests, particularly in livestock production. It did not take long, twenty years in general, when there were insects that became increasingly resistant to DDT. DDT also had its affects upon pollution of land, water supplies, and bodies of water until its use was banned.

One of us attended a science teachers convention in which a speaker stated how beneficial earthworms are to soil such as in providing natural fertilizer from body wastes, aeration of the soil, and richness of the soil. The speaker perceived the situation from one perception only and that was the negative effects of using pesticides and herbicides which kill many, many earthworms. The earthworm certainly provides soil with its numerous benefits to be sure. However, the income factor for farmers is also involved in that pests and weeds destroy domesticated plants. A highly complex problem is involved. With adequate background information, pupils with teacher guidance may brainstorm possible solutions to the dilemma of using agricultural chemicals to destroy pests and weeds as compared to using other procedures to minimize yield damage to farm crops. Other procedures might include the use of insects which feed upon pests that destroy farm crops. To control weeds, brightly coloured flowers which attract pests have been used by gardeners, thus protecting valuable garden crops for human consumption. However, efforts so far in controlling pests and weeds have been only successful in a minor way.

To vary procedures of instruction mentioned in this manuscript, a learning stations approach may be used in the curriculum on natural disasters. An adequate number of stations need to be in the offing. Each station has concrete, semiconcrete, and abstract learning activities from which learners may choose sequentially to pursue. There are more tasks at the different stations than what any one learner can complete. Those tasks not possessing perceived purpose by the pupil may be omitted. The pupil is the chooser. The teacher assists and helps each pupil to accomplish as much as possible. The tasks at each station should be meaningful, interesting, emphasize a balance between individual and group endeavours, as well as possess challenge.

Learners sequence or order their very own activities and experiences. An activity centred curriculum in science is an end result.

Ediger and Bhaskara Rao (1996) stress the importance of having a variety of learning opportunities in teaching science for the following reasons:

1. pupils have different learning styles;
2. different levels of achievement in science exist within any class of pupils;
3. not all pupils, of course, benefit equally from the same activity;
4. teachers have different teaching styles;
5. selected learning activities capture the interests of pupils more than do other kinds of experiences;
6. individuals desire new experiences;
7. monotony in activities hinders pupils in developing motivation toward learning.

Philosophy of Science Education

A study of diverse philosophies of education might well assist teachers to make quality decisions pertaining to current events in the science curriculum. Ediger (1995) wrote:

Diverse philosophical schools of thought in science are in evidence to develop and implement lessons plans and units in science.

Experimentalism emphasizes the use of problem solving experiences for pupil. Flexible steps in problems solving involve

1. Identifying the problem.
2. Gathering data to solve the identified problem.
3. Developing a hypothesis, directly based to the obtained data and in answer to the problem.
4. Testing the hypothesis.
5. Revising the hypothesis, if evidence warrants.

Experimentalism emphasizes that real live problems be identified by pupils. The problems come directly from society. In society, earthquakes, hurricanes, tornadoes, volcanic eruptions, among other natural phenomena occur. Out of these scenes and situations, problems arise and are identified, such as "What makes for the happening of earthquakes?" Information needs to be gathered to answer the problem or question. An answer, tentative in nature, is then developed. The answer, a hypothesis, is then checked against further content, secured from a variety of reference sources. Modification of the original answer of hypotheses may then be needed.

Idealism, as a philosophy of education, emphasizes an idea centred curriculum. Science then becomes a part of the general education curriculum. A subject centred, not an activity centred philosophy, is then in evidence. Diverse academic disciplines such as zoology, botany, physics, astronomy, biology, chemistry, and geology provide subject matter for ongoing units of study. Textbooks, workbooks, worksheets, and a few selected audiovisual aids provide content for pupils. Universal ideas or generalizations in science units need to be achieved by pupils. The teacher needs to be a true academician and scholar to stimulate pupil learning.

Realism, as a third philosophy of education, advocates the use of precise, measurable objectives. Realist believe the real world can be known in whole or part as it truly is. What pupils achieve in each science unit can be measured. The real world of natural phenomena can be stated in precise, measurable objectives. A variety of concrete learning activities, in particular, should be provided for pupils to attain the precise ends. Semiconcrete as well as abstract experiences also should be in the offing. After instruction, it is observable and measurable if an objective has been achieved by pupils.

Existentialism, as a fourth philosophy of education, emphasizes the learner, himself or herself, being heavily involved in deciding what (the objectives) to learn, as well as the means (learning activities) in ongoing science units of study.

Thus, a learning centres philosophy may be emphasized. More centres and tasks for learners to pursue are in evidence than what can be completed. Each pupil may then sequentially choose which tasks to complete, as well as which to omit. Pupils individually are involved in making these decisions. The teacher develops the centres for learner interaction. Better yet, pupil/teacher planning may be used to develop the centres and their inherent tasks.

In supervising student teachers and cooperating teachers in the public schools, we have observed the following current events items in science emphasized in each of the above named philosophies:

1. *Experimentalism:* In an ongoing lesson, pupils identified problems such as *(a)* why did Iran experience a major earthquake this past weekend? *(b)* How is the strength of earthquakes measured?
2. *Idealism:* A teacher determined topic for discussion with pupil involvement stressing in an ongoing unit *(a)* the causes of hurricanes and their after affects. *(b)* the differences between hurricanes and tornadoes.
3. *Realism:* The science teacher stating prior to implementing the lesson on the following two precise objectives pupils are to achieve: *(a)* The pupil will list in writing three causes of major floods in the environment. *(b)* The pupil will write a fifty word paragraph on ways of preventing flood damage.
4. *Existentialism:* Pupils choosing what to study in a unit through teacher/learner planning. These areas, for example, might include *(a)* What may be done to help people care for each other when a natural disaster such as a cyclone occurs. *(b)* How might the United States annual budget be changed so that the needs of people are met in times of emergency when destruction from natural forces occurs?

Our recommendations here are that current events in science emphasize problem solving. Experimentalism then should hold sway. Thus subject matter acquired when stressing idealism, content achieved from attaining measurably stated objectives (realism), and pupil/teacher planning procedures (existentialism) may all be used to identify and solve problems. Why is problem solving important? In life's situations, people face problems which need identification and necessary solutions. Each solution appears to be tentative and will need revisions as evidence indicates. In everyday situations then, individuals and groups experience problems continually which need some kind of answer.

There are current events papers written especially for the grade level pupils are in presently. These present items pertaining to natural disasters, among other human related factors.

Newspapers written for pupils have an intended audience and that is the learner himself/herself. Many problems in word recognition have been taken care of when a child centred paper has been written, but to provide for individual needs, selected learners will still need assistance in identifying unknown words. A few pupils will also need guidance in understanding the meaning of important words. Current events papers can have much appeal to learners providing that the teacher assists pupils in achieving background information prior to reading these weekly/monthly newspapers.

To assist pupil learning in discussions after having read the current events items, the following guidelines need to be stressed by teachers:

1. Each pupil needs to stay on the topic being discussed and not digress to other information.
2. Learners must respect the thinking of each discussion participant.
3. It is important to listen carefully to the ideas of others in the group.
4. All should be actively engaged in the discussion, but no one dominate the interactions.
5. Content presented should be evaluated in an atmosphere of respect and trust.

6. Participants need to speak clearly and accurately in terms of concepts, generalizations, main ideas, and facts presented.
7. Valid and reliable conclusions should be drawn from each discussion.
8. Chairpersons may be chosen by the teacher with rotation procedures. Leadership might also emerge within a group without a chairperson.

Group/committee endeavours may follow listening to a radio news broadcast on natural catastrophes in the environment. These may be cassette recorded by the teacher in the home setting so that only relevant information is played to pupils. The teacher may also videotape, with the VCR, vital current events items from TV broadcasts in the home setting. These may be played in the classroom with proper readiness provided by the science teacher. Daily newspaper items as well as weekly news items from reputable magazines might well provide relevant information on natural disasters and means used to prevent these occurrences from doing damage. The latest data sources should also be heavily used and involved in the science curriculum such as Internet and computer packages. To achieve optimally in science current events, pupils need to experience quality reference sources using a hands-on approach.

Organisation of the Science Current Events Curriculum

There are several approaches that may be used by the teacher to organise the current events programme in science. First, the teacher may take time at the beginning of each class session to discuss news articles that pupils have brought in for discussion. Thus, a pupil might, for example, have brought in a news item about an avalanche that caused much destruction in a village in Switzerland. The temperature readings there were much warmer for that season than usual causing the snow and ice to melt above on the mountains. The result was a massive amount of snow and ice that came crashing down onto houses in the village. Or a pupil brought to the class a news clipping about the flooding of the Ohio River causing home evacuations and much property damage due to the mighty force of the rushing flood waters. A third pupil brought into the classroom and reported on a volcanic eruption in the Philippines. These happenings occurred simultaneously. There are enough natural disasters occurring which could provide an entire unit in science for pupils to study. These occurrences may be placed around a would map with a coloured piece of yarn connecting the place of the geographical location with the news clipping. Geography and the science curriculum are then correlated and taught as being related. Several of my students teachers and there cooperating teachers whom one of the authors have supervised in the public schools believe very strongly in bringing in humanitarian efforts used to alleviate the resulting human suffering from natural disasters. Historical efforts in assisting the unfortunate during times of natural disasters bring in a study of history integrated with the science curriculum. With the above examples given an entire science unit may be taught entitled "Natural Disasters and Their Consequences".

A second approach in organising the science current events curriculum is to discuss with pupils news items as they relate to the ongoing unit of study. Thus, if pupils, for example, are studying a unit on "Preserving Wildlife", current events items may emphasize sanctuaries for bald eagles, an endangered species. Also recently, wolves from Alaska were released into a designated area in the state of Wyoming. Wolves formerly had a niche in that state but had become extinct until a new pack from Alaska was released in Wyoming. An issue that can provide for higher levels of cognition which might be discussed here is the point of view of cattle ranchers in Wyoming versus those of wildlife advocates in restoring an area to its original state. We have observed pupils with teacher guidance doing much research from a variety of reference sources to understand opposing sides in a dispute. Intrinsic motivation seems to be in evidence here.

A third approach in organising the current events is to stress the separate subjects curriculum. Here, pupils are encouraged to bring news items to class if they relate to the ongoing unit in science or not. There are excellent reasons for emphasizing the separate subjects procedure in organising the current events programme in science. Thus, there are vital news happenings in the world of science that have no relationship to the ongoing unit of study being taught. Then too, there are not an adequate number of science news items that relate so that an entire unit may be taught. At the same time, the isolated news item brought to class is highly relevant and should receive adequate attention in class as soon as possible. We have observed in different classrooms which have a quality programme of science in the news and yet the items are not related to the present unit being taught. We would like to offer the following suggestions for implementing a good current events programme. These suggestions are the following:

1. pupils should volunteer to bring into the classroom setting news items pertaining to science. If there is a lack of voluntary participation, the science teacher may require pupils to collect and have well in mind relevant news items pertaining to science;
2. the teacher(s) need to reward pupil participation by praising positive efforts;
3. learners should understand and attach meaning to news items presented to classmates;
4. each news item needs to be evaluated using critical and creative thinking as well as problem solving procedures. To think critically, pupils need to separate facts from opinions, fantasy from reality, as well as detect bias. With creative thinking, pupils come up with new, novel ideas when predicting what might happen in the future based on knowledge. Unique ideas are needed in any endeavour since creativity is necessary in response to problem areas. Too frequently, the tried and true are stressed and this may not work in a new situation involving problem solving;

5. pupils should be encouraged to use what has been learned. If knowledge is not used, it might be forgotten. Also, use made of what has been learned makes for relevance in the current events science curriculum.

There are many uses that can be made of any vital current events item studied. The following have been observed in different classrooms and appear to work well:

1. pupils in a committee collaboratively working on a mural to portray content learned. Thus three or four pupils worked on a mural four feet by five in dimension. Planning together what to show using a variety of art media stress a problem solving approach. Thus each pupil showed one of the following: plate tectonics in art form; a hurricane with its destructive path; a fault with different layers of rock; and sheet/gulley erosion;
2. three pupils in a committee made a model volcano using wadded newspaper for the core with a potted empty meat can for the opening at the top of the model volcano. The outside of the volcano was finished with a plaster of Paris mix to make for a realistic portrayal. The plaster of Paris dries quickly and pupils need to work quickly to give the model an identifiable lifelike appearance. Tempera paint may be used to give the model a natural like appearance in its final form. Ammonium dichromate crystals may be put into the empty potted meat can. These crystals, obtained from a scientific supply company, should then be ignited. A model volcanic eruption occurs. There needs to be ample ventilation in the classroom when doing this experiment;
3. pupils developing and presenting a simulated radio newscast on recent natural disasters, locally and nationally. Careful writing and editing of the news is important. A pupil playing the role of the reporter may read the news to the class as would be done in regular newscasts on the radio;

4. three pupils in a committee researching and completing a written report on natural disasters in farming. The science teacher assist these learners to secure relevant information on drouth, hail, and excessive rainfall. Oral reports to classmates on each of these disasters may reveal to pupils what happens when there is a lack of moisture for growing crops, when hail destroys farm crops in a minute or two, and when fields are too wet for seeding or for harvesting;
5. pupils may plan and play roles of *Famous Scientists* when studying this science unit. Much background information is needed to develop the creative dramatics activity. Thus, individual pupils may play roles of well known scientists such as Louis Pasteur, Galileo, and Antony Leeuvenhoek. The presentation may be given to classmates and pupils in other classrooms, as well as to parents invite to the classroom.

The above five examples of how to put knowledge of current events in science to use by pupils are given as models. There are numerous other ideas that can be used by teachers to have pupils apply what has been learned. Shepardson and Britsch (1997) favour pupil journal writing as an excellent means of having pupils apply what has been learned:

Children's observations are essential for learning, but unfortunately they are often downplayed in the science teaching process. It is from science observations that the child begins to construct scientific understanding. Children may, however, have difficulties in observing differences, erroneously recording deductions as observations. To assess the quality of these observations, teachers can analyse journals for the following indicators:

1. actual observations versus deductions;
2. level of detail (qualitative and quantitative);
3. notations of similarities and differences;
4. comparisons between phenomenon in terms of position (spatial) and time (change);

5. and accurate, careful descriptions...

To assess the quality of children's observations, specific scoring rubrics need to be developed based on the nature of the activity and the importance of the children's observations in the teaching/learning process.

In Closing

There are numerous natural disasters which need to be emphasized in the science curriculum. A key concept here is relevancy when choosing which news items to pursue. An interdisciplinary curriculum incorporates social studies, mathematics, and language arts. Pupils need assistance to understand that knowledge is related. Retention of subject matter learned improves when pupils can perceive that current events is related to diverse academic disciplines. Ample opportunities should be provided for pupil to work collaboratively with others in the school setting. Problem solving and learner decision making need to be stressed since life itself consists of solving problems and choosing from among alternatives to make decisions. Relevant objectives, learning opportunities, and appraisal procedures should be in the offing for all pupils in units pertaining to natural disasters in the environment. A good current events curriculum in science is a must.

Pertaining to current events, Schuncke (1988) wrote:

There are four basic questions that should be considered in a current events discussion:

1. What does the news item say? Here, your job is to determine that the children are aware of the basic message contained in the news item. You'll want to insure that they know the facts surrounding an event, the who, what, when, where, why, and possibly how.
2. What does it mean? Knowing the facts... does not necessarily mean that the children understand it. Therefore, you will next need to determine their level of comprehension, how they interpret the item, and

what inferences they can make about it. You'll want to make certain they have, at least, a basic understanding of what's going on.

3. Why is it important? The question, or a related one, should be used to help children probe the effect of an event—on the children themselves, on others, and on the world.

4. How does it relate to me? Here children can be assisted to examine their roles as citizens—of a community, state, nation, and world—to determine if the importance of an event requires some action on their part. Often the question can lead to decision making, valuing, and social action in their part.

REFERENCES

Butler, Gene, et. al. (1996). "Earthquakes Online," *The Science Teacher,* Vol. 63. No. 9, Pages 31-32.

Ediger, Marlow, and D. Bhaskara Rao (1996). *Science Curriculum.* New Delhi: Discovery Publishing House, Pages 40-41.

Ediger, Marlow (1995). "Designing Science Units of Study," *Social Science,* Vol. 33, No. 1, Pages 14-15.

Schuncke, George M., *Elementary Social Studies.* New York: The Macmillan Publishing, Page 72.

Shepardson, Deniel P., and Susan J. Britsch (1997). "Children's Science Journals: Tools for Teaching, Learning and Assessing," *Science and Children,* Vol. 34, No. 5, Page 17.

3

Excellence in the Science Curriculum

Each person lives in a world of science. The natural environment affects all of us. It operates in terms of scientific theories, principles, and laws. Pupils in the public school setting need to achieve relevant goals in science. These goals should be attainable, meaningful, and possess purpose for the learner. The *Show Me Standards* (1996) list the following science objectives for pupil achievement in Missouri schools:

In Science, students in Missouri public schools will acquire a solid foundation which includes knowledge of

1. properties and principles of matter and energy;
2. properties and principles of force and motion;
3. characteristics and interactions of living organisms;
4. changes of ecosystems and interactions of organisms with their environment;
5. processes (such as plate movement, water cycle, air flow) and interactions of Earth's biosphere, atmosphere, lithosphere, and hydrosphere;
6. composition and structure of the universe and the motions of objects within it;

7. processes of scientific inquiry (such as formulating and testing hypotheses);
8. impact of science, technology and human activity on resources and the environment.

Each of the above named objectives should be emphasized within a related, designatd unit of study. The objectives might also be written more precisely, if desired, so that it can be measured if a pupil has/had not achieve each stated end of instruction. There are states in the United States that mandate measurably stated objectives. Other states have a more open-ended approach in allowing leeway in writing objectives. We recommend that objectives not be written so precisely that facts only are emphasized on tests to appraise pupil achievement. The following objective stresses pupils memorizing facts: the pupil will list in writing the names of ten arthropods. Then too, objectives can be so broadly stated that they become meaningless such as "The pupil will learn science." This objective certainly lacks clarity in terms of what will be taught and evaluated to determine pupil achievement.

To improve the quality of life for each person, a problem solving approach should be emphasized in ongoing lessons and units in science. With problem solving, change occurs from what is to what should be in science.

Diverse schools of philosophical thought will be discussed and how each might relate to improve the science curriculum.

Realism in the Science Curriculum

A science teacher who is a realist emphasizes that one can know the real world, in whole or in part, as it truly is. This mind then does not modify or change what is being perceived. Tillman, Berofsky, and O' Connor (1971) wrote, "Most people when they think about the objects of perception, would say that they perceive a world of objects which is external to them and which exists independently of their perception of it. This view is called realism".

Since the external world is perceived the way it is in actuality, specific objective of instruction can be determined by scientists and science educators for pupils to achieve. Each objective must be relevant and is a part of the whole that can be know by the learner. Thus in geology, biology, chemistry, physics, and astronomy, among other academic, disciplines, measurably stated objectives of instruction need to be emphasized in teaching and learning in the science curriculum. With quality learning opportunities selected by the science teacher, pupils either achieve or do not achieve the specific objective(s) as a result of instruction. Measuring pupil achievement in learning stresses what pupils have learned what was stated in each objective. Realists desire observable results in learning from pupils. The results are verifiable regardless of which teacher is appraising learner progress. The verification principle is very important to teachers of science who adhere to realism as a philosophy of instruction.

Skinner (1979) was a leading advocate in stressing precise objectives for pupil attainment. Reinforcement is emphasized to reward correct/good responses in learning. Observable, measurable results are obtained from what pupils have achieved. Guesswork is not involved, but per cents, standard deviations, quartile deviations, grade equivalents, and percentile ranks emphasize how well each pupil is doing in the area of science instruction. Numerical results of pupil achievement in science is wanted by the realist teacher. Scores from tests; objective evaluations of science experiments and demonstrations performed by pupils; ratings given to learner performance as well as responses to questions oral reports, port folios, and related papers written in which interobserver reliability is in evidence, present data as to how well pupils are achieving. These procedures qualify as objective means of appraising learner progress.

Mager (1972) stressed the importance of writing objectives so they are operationalized. Objectives are then specific and clear to teachers, pupils, and other interested persons. Learning opportunities may be chosen and aligned with the stated objectives. Appraisal procedures used to determine pupil achievement are also aligned with the objectives. Quality validity and reliability are then in the offing. A pupil reveals if he/she attained or did not attain a stated objective. The realist science teacher wishes to know if pupils individually are or are not achieving objectives of instruction. The results may then be reported to parents in a very precise way.

Prior to instruction, the teachers may announce to pupils which objectives will be emphasized in the science lesson or unit. The pupil knows exactly what will be expected in terms of knowledge or skills to be obtained. The involved pupil should have more confidence in learning when realizing what the instructor's expectations are. The science teacher might desire to arrange the objectives in an ascending order of complexity. A logical sequence follows since the teacher sequences objectives in science for the pupil to achieve.

Advantages given for emphasizing realism as a philosophy of instruction are the following:

1. teachers may realize how successful they are in teaching since results from pupil learning are clear and observable;
2. objectives, learning activities, and evaluation procedures are interrelated in that the learning activities and the evaluation procedures must harmonize with the stated objectives. Thus, for example, it becomes easier to choose learning activities than otherwise would be the case due to the harmony needed between these activities and the stated objectives;
3. effective schools research states that pupils achieve better if there is a clear relationship between the learning activities and the evaluation procedures with that of the objectives of science instruction (Edmonds, 1982).

Disadvantages given for emphasizing realism as a philosophy of education stress the fragmented knowledge that pupils may learn since each objective achieved emphasizes parts of a whole. The teacher controls the science curriculum since he/she determines the objectives, learning opportunities, and evaluation procedures; pupils are not involved here in decision making. The products of instruction in science are emphasized, leaving little room for processes such as abstract thinking which is rather difficult to measure.

Examples of precise objectives for pupils to achieve in science are the following:

1. The pupil will write a paragraph indicating seven animals involved in a food chain.
2. The pupil will make a drawing showing ten animals in a forest food web and their interactions.
3. The pupil will list in writing the names of five parasites and their respective hosts.
4. The pupil will define each of the following: producers, consumers, decomposers, symbiosis, and an aquatic/land community.

Experimentalism in the Science Curriculum

Experimentalists stress a problem solving approach in the curriculum. They emphasize that individuals cannot know the real world as it truly is. Individuals, however obtain experiences of this reality. With experiences, changes occur in one's thinking and believing. A changing world makes for problematic situations. Problems need identification and solutions sought. In the science curriculum, pupils with teacher guidance select a problem within an ongoing lesson or unit of study. The problem needs to be adequately delimited so that meaning and understanding is involved. An hypothesis is developed directly related to the stated problem. Information from a variety of sources is used by learners to arrive at a tentative solution. Experimentalists believe all knowledge to be tentative, not absolute.

The result might well involved changing and modifying the original hypotheses. The new hypothesis is then tried out in a concrete situation (Geiger, 1955). Problem solving may be used in all curriculum areas and in life itself. Knowledge here is used to solve problems and is not an end in and of itself. The practical and the utilitarian are emphasized within the framework of problem solving: knowledge secured from a variety of sources has an application dimension. Knowledge then is useful to solve problems in a changing world, science included (Ediger 1995).

Experimentalists emphasize that school and society are one, not separate entities. Since groups in society select and solve problems, pupils in committees also need to be involved in cooperative learning stressing problem solving. School and society are one, not separate entities. Dewey (1915) is still very widely recognized as a leading advocate of experimentalism in teaching and learning. In integrating the learner with the self as well as with the societal arena, he advocated four characteristics of pupils which have wide implications for the teaching of science. These are that pupils possess the social impulse in that they desire to work together with others in the curriculum; the constructive impulse in which learners like to learn by doing, not being passive individuals; the investigative and experimentalism inclination whereby pupils desire to learn by discovery rather than being told and lectured; and the creative or expressive impulse, rather than have rigid formal expectations for achievement.

Advantages given in emphasizing experimentalism as a philosophy of teaching science are the following:

1. pupil interest in science becomes paramount when they with teacher assistance identify problem areas. Interest in learning makes for effort in achieving;
2. very young pupils in early primary grades may be involved in problem solving experiences (Ediger, 1994);
3. problem solving is useful in all curriculum areas and in life itself when problems are selected and solutions sought.

Disadvantages of using experimentalism as a philosophy of education include problem selection being too difficult as well as problem solving may not be a favourite style and way of learning for a few pupils. Also motivation may be lacking for some pupils to identify and solve problems.

The following are examples of possible problems for pupils to solve:

1. How do animals adapt to their natural environment?
2. How do cells differ in size and shape to fulfil their unique functions? How are cells similar in features possessed?
3. How do unicellular and multicellular organisms differ from each other?
4. Which life processes do all living things perform?

Pertaining to John Dewey's philosophy of experimentalism, Meyer (1949) wrote:

All of this, of course, depends upon in no small way on thinking. For Dewey, however, thinking becomes significant only when applied to life situations. It is, he has said, "an instrumentality used by man in adjusting himself to the practical situations in life". Or to phrase it more simply, human beings think in order to live. Because of this stimulus, which has its basis in biology and sociology, it is impossible—it is absurd—to interpret life in a systematic and abstract way. Since, moreover, Dewey holds that life is in constant flux, it is impossible to solve problems with any degree of finality for the problems of tomorrow will be different from those of today.

As for the problem of knowledge, Dewey believes that knowledge and true experience is functional. What is this thing for? What is its use? Is a coal mine a physical deposit or does to have function? and if so, what is it? Such are the questions that help to give meaning to one's experience; but such questions cannot be answered without antecedent action. Action must precede knowledge. Whatever knowledge we possess has resulted from our activities, our efforts to survive, to obtain food, shelter, and clothing. Only that which has been organised into our disposition so as to enable us to adapt to our environment to meet our needs and to adapt our aims and desires to the situation in which we exist is really knowledge.

Idealism in the Science Curriculum

Idealists believe that one can receive ideas about the real world only. Thus one cannot know the real world as it truly is independent of the observer. Mental development in idealism becomes of utmost importance since an idea centred world is in evidence. Mind is real and needs development. As a leading idealist still quoted widely presently, Horne (1932) stressed the importance of the use of reason and rational thought in arriving at truth. Concepts and generalisations or universals such as justice, truth, goodness, ethics, and beauty have always existed and can be discovered by human beings. These universals are a priori, to an idealist, in that they have existed prior to human experience.

A subject centred curriculum in science is of paramount importance. In science lessons and units of study, pupils should achieve vital concepts, and generalizations. Depth teaching is needed to cultivate the intellect in guiding pupils achievement in science. A multimedia approach in learning is needed to assist pupils to achieve abstract ideas in science. The abstract to an idealist is superior to the concrete and semiconcrete in learning. The concrete and semiconcrete facets of learning in science are salient to the degree that learners attain the abstract such as vital facts, concepts, and generalizations in ongoing lessons and units of study. Since reading and writing, in particular, stress abstract learnings, they should not be minimized in the science curriculum.

To emphasize a subject centred curriculum as idealists recommend, an academically inclined teacher needs to teach in a scholarly way so that objectives stressing intellectual goals are attained by pupils. Blanchard (1964) wrote

The aim of thought from its very beginning, we saw, was at understanding. To understand anything meant to apprehend it in a system that rendered it necessary. The ideal of complete understanding would be achieved only when the system that rendered it necessary was not a system that itself was fragmentary and therefore contingent, but one that was all-inclusive and so organised internally that every part was linked to every other by intelligible necessity.

Advantages given for emphasizing idealism as a philosophy of teaching science include the following:

1. pupils are to achieve significant subject matter. Idealism emphasizes the acquisition of vital content in science that pupils need to attain. Use made of knowledge in science need to emphasize what is just to all, what is truthful, what is good in its application, what will truly stress ethical dimensions, and that which has beauty in its aesthetical areas;
2. many pupils may be motivated to learn when an academic approach to learn science is stressed. This might be especially appealing to the gifted and talented learners in science. All pupils need motivation to achieve and learn in science;
3. the abstract in idealism is preferred to the concrete and semiconcrete; relevant concepts, and generalizations, and other universals emphasize abstract goals in science teaching. Idealist advocate wholeness in knowledge, not fragmentation. Knowledge is related in all of its manifestations.

Disadvantages given for idealism as a philosophy in teaching and learning include minimizing a hands on approach in learning science since the focal point of teaching is to have pupils develop well intellectually; placing emphasis upon universals much more so than specifics—the latter is salient in pupils arriving at conclusions such as in science experiments; and integrating of knowledge to the point where science as a discipline is not as clearly defined as it might be. Idealists tend to stress that which goes beyond the five senses. Thus metaphysics and the a priori are salient to an idealist.

Quality sequence in science might be slighted when abstract phases of learning are more prized more highly than the concrete and semiconcrete. Most educators presently recommend a sequence of concrete, semiconcrete, to the abstract in teaching-learning situations. Quite similar in sequence, Bruner (1968) advocated using manipulative materials such as objects and items; followed by iconic materials such as audiovisual materials which are one step removed from the manipulative phase; and then symbolic activities which stresses the abstract including reading and writing.

Objectives in science, according to idealism as a philosophy of education, might well stress the following universal topics:

1. monerans such as bacteria and blue green algae. Monerans are prokaryotes in that they have no true nucleus. They consist of producers, consumers, and decomposers. A few move around whereas others are stationary;
2. protists, such as paramecium, euglenas, diatoms, and cribaria. Protists are unicellular and have a true nucleus. With a true nucleus, protists are eukaryotes, and are producers as well as consumers;
3. fungi, such as mushrooms and bread molds. Most fungi are multicellular. Since fungi do not contain chlorophyll, most are decomposers with a few being consumers;
4. plants, such as mosses, liverworts, ferns, and seed plants. Plants are eukaryotes and are producers. Plants do not move from one place to another.

Pertaining to idealism, Bigge (1982) wrote:

The heart of idealism is the belief that basic reality consists of ideas, thoughts, minds, or substantive selves, not physical matter. Since priority is given to minds, minds have bodies, but bodies do not have minds. Idealism carries with its view the idea of subsistence (the superexistence) of God, who also is basically mind or self. The universe is an expression of intelligence and will; its order is due to an eternal, spiritual reality. For idealists, people are good-active substantive minds; they are absolutely real selves endowed with free will or genuine moral choice. This philosophy has ancient roots; it dates back to Socrates (469-399 BC) and Plato (427-347 B.C).

Idealism really is idea-ism. The source of this title is based on Platonic thought. For Plato, ideas only are genuinely real; they consisted of immaterial essences. That which people perceive is a shadow of reality; each thing that they perceive gets its existence from its Thingness; an idea. A book is a book because of its being more or less an imperfect replica of Bookness, a woman is a woman because she is a replica of Womanness. Plato's assumed world of "eternal varities" consisted of the True, the Good, and the Beautiful.

We can trace the development of idealism by listing some of the leading philosophers who have contributed to this position and stating a leading idea that each has contributed to this philosophy. Socrates believed that children are born with knowledge already in their minds, but they needed help to recall this innate knowledge. Plato contributed to the idea of Ideas, which are the universal forms of all existing things and are the essence of reality. St. Augustine (350-430) held a dualistic (mind-body) force of goodness.

Existentialism and the Science Curriculum

Existentialists believe that one exists first and then finds his/her purposes in life; there are no standards to guide human begins other than those developed by the human race. Most existentialists advocate that people are condemned to be free with no a priori standards in life. Individuals then make or break themselves due to the kind of society wanted. Each person chooses and makes choices continually. To be human is to choose. If a person permits the self to have someone else makes one's own decisions, then the individual ceases to be human.

Combs (1972) stresses that the way individuals perceive a situation will assist in determining how the individual will behave. Perception is unique to the individual. Each person decides upon what is true, judges what is good, and decides upon plans of action. The science curriculum then must provide opportunities for pupils individually to decide what to learn, that is the objectives of instruction. The pupil needs to be heavily involved in selecting learning opportunities as well as methods of determining progress. The teacher is a guide and encourages pupil learning. The teacher, however, does not lecture nor determine the science curriculum for the individual pupil. A learning centres approach in teaching science may then be emphasized. Here, there are an adequate number of centres with quality tasks for learners at each centre. There needs to be more tasks than what a pupil can complete so that individual sequential choices may truly be made. A psychological, not logical, science curriculum is then in evidence. Each pupil may select tasks based on personal needs, interests, and purposes. The choice to be made is up to the individual pupil. If tasks do not meet personal needs of the involved learner, he/she might plan with the teacher what has merit and value to the pupil. A contract system might also be implemented in which the pupil with teacher guidance selects tasks to put into a contract for completion. The learner himself/herself is responsible for choices made. The individual perceives what is good and has quality. Knowledge is subjective, not objective to the existentialists. For example, in a values clarification session, the pupil determines what is moral in terms of uses made of science and technology; the teacher has a difficult position as a stimulator and of one who encourages pupil learning. Being humane in an absurd environment is a major goal for pupil achievement in existentialists thought and thinking.

Within an existentialist science curriculum, through pupil/teacher planning a learner may select topics such as the following to pursue:

1. How do pesticides and herbicides help or hinder the natural environment? This question pertains to curbing insects and weed growth for the raising of farm crops versus possible contamination of soil and water.
2. How does one deal with animals in a humane way? This question stresses what to do with surplus dogs and cats roaming an area, as well as using animals for food and for scientific experiments.
3. How can the natural environment be used for development so that adequate numbers of jobs are available for workers versus the destruction of natural habitats for wildlife?
4. How can the needs of individuals be met as well as those in the societal arenas? This raises the question of the individual versus the larger group in a community, state, nation, and the world.

Alston and Brandt (1978) write the following direct quote of Jean Paul Sartre, a late leading existentialists:

Man is nothing else but what he makes of himself. Such is the first principle of existentialism. It is also what is called subjectivity, the name we are labelled with when charges are brought against us. But what do we mean by this, if not that man has a greater dignity than a stone or table? For we mean that man first exists, that is, that man first of all is the being who hurls himself into the future and who is conscious of imagining himself being in the future. Man is at the start a plan which is aware of itself, rather than a patch of moss, a piece of garbage, or a cauliflower; nothing exists prior to this plan; there is nothing in heaven; man will be what he will have planned to be. Not what he will want to be. Because by the word 'will' we generally mean a conscious decision, which is subsequent to what we have made of ourselves. I may want to belong to a political party, write a book, get married; but all that is only a manifestation of an earlier, more spontaneous choice that is called 'will'. But if existence really precedes essence, man is responsible for what he is. Thus, existentialism's first move is to make every man aware of what he is and to make the full responsibility of his existence rest upon him. And when we say that a man is responsible for individuality, but that he is responsible for all men.

The Psychology of Education

Principles of learning from the psychology of learning give direction to the science teacher in teaching-learning situations in ongoing lessons and units of study. Ediger (1994) lists the following criteria upon which educational psychologists agree should be followed by teachers:

1. meaningful learning experiences should be provided pupils in the curriculum;
2. interesting content and skills should be offered in lessons and units of study;
3. purpose needs to be established within pupils for learning;
4. quality sequence for pupil learning is a must;
5. rational balance among knowledge, skills, and attitudinal objectives is important in the instructional arena.

In Summary

Science teachers need to select tenets from the philosophy of education which stress pupils attaining vital content, abilities, and attitudes. In reviewing the different philosophies of education discussed in this paper, the following is salient from each philosophy:

1. clarity in objectives of science instruction, carefully selected, as recommended by realists. However, it is important to avoid fragmenting knowledge obtained by pupils;
2. problem solving procedures as recommended by experimentalists. Life in society emphasizes the importance of being able to solve personal and social problems;

3. major concepts and generalizations, an universals in science, advocated by idealists;
4. decision making opportunities in science as recommended by existentialists. Each person needs to learn to make decisions.

We believe that a problem solving philosophy encompasses the other three philosophies. We recommend problem solving as a major philosophy of education to emphasize in teaching science due to its relevance in the curriculum and in life itself. Problems abound and need solutions. Knowledge acquired then is instrumental or useful in problems to be solved which are selected by pupils with teacher guidance.

Ediger and Bhaskara Rao (1996) wrote the following in summarizing different psychologies of teaching.

Comparisons were made among the following models in teaching science:

1. problem solving with teacher guidance;
2. behaviourism with its predetermined precise objectives for student attainment;
3. humanism and its emphasis upon students selecting sequential activities from among alternatives;
4. the structure of knowledge with key concepts and generalizations identified by academicians in their respective areas of specialization. Science teachers assist students to achieve these structural ideas inductively using methods and procedures of scientists in a science laboratory setting;
5. stimulus—response learning of students in which a specific response is associated with a precise stimulus.

The writers advocate a problem solving approach be utilized in teaching science. From a stimulating learning environment in science, students with teacher guidance identify and solve vital problems. Problem solving skills are useful in all academic areas, as well as in the societal arena. Behaviourism, humanism, the structure of knowledge, and stimulus—response learning may be emphasized within the framework of problem solving situations. Subject matter in science may then be utilized in the problem solving science curriculum.

REFERENCES

Alston, William P., and Richard W. Brandt (1978). *The Problems of Philosophy*, Third Edition. Boston: Allyn and Bacon, Inc., Pages 257-258.

Bigge, Morris (1982). *Educational Philosophies for Teachers*, Columbus, Ohio: Charles E. Merrill Publishing Company, Pages 25-26.

Blanchard, Brand (1964). *The Nature of Thought*. New York: Humanities Press, 492-517.

Bruner, Jerome (1968). *Toward A Theory of Instruction*. Cambridge, Massachusetts: Harvard University Press.

Combs, Arthur (1972). *Educational Objectives: Beyond Behavioural Objectives*. Washington, DC: Association for Supervision and Curriculum Development.

Dewey, John (1915). *School and Society*. Chicago: University of Chicago Press.

Ediger, Marlow (1995). Demonstration Teaching in the Schools. *Education*, 114, 371-372.

Ediger, Marlow (1994). Mathematics, Problem Solving, and the Young Learner. *The Primary Teacher*, 19, 34-37.

Ediger, Marlow. Early Field Experiences in Teacher Education. *College Student Journal*, 28. 302-306.

Ediger, Marlow, and D. Bhaskara Rao. *Science Curriculum. New* Delhi, India: Discovery Publishing House, Page 117.

Edmonds, Ron (1982). Programs of School Improvement: An Overview. *Educational Leadership,* December, Volume 4.

Geiger, George W. (1955). An Experimentalist Approach to Education. *Modern Philosophies and Education*. Chicago, Illinois: National Society for the Study of Education, 54, 137-174.

Horne, Herman Harrell (1932). *The Democratic Philosophy of Education*. New York: The Macmillan Company, 325-340.

Mager, Robert F. (1972). *Goal Analysis*. Belmont, California: Fearon Publishers.

Missouri Department of Elementary and Secondary Education (1996), *Show Me Standards*, Jefferson City, Missouri.

Meyer, Adolph E. (1949). *The Development of Education in the Twentieth Century*. Englewood Cliffs, New Jersey: Prentice-Hall, Inc., Pages 42-43.

Skinner, B.F. (1979). *Beyond Freedom and Dignity*. New York: Alfred Knopf, Inc.

Tillman, Frank A., and Others (1971). *Introductory Philosophy*. New York: Harper and Row, Page 550.

4

Leadership in the Science Curriculum

Leadership is needed in schools to overcome problems in the school setting. Richardson and others (1989) emphasized that principals be proactive and not reactive persons. Thus problems tend to be identified before they happen rather than reacting to crises situations only. Ediger (1993) stressed the importance of administrators and supervisors being highly knowledgeable about the curriculum in providing for optimal learner achievement. Much parental dissatisfaction might well be avoided if leadership capabilities were used to guide each pupil to attain as much as possible.

Knowledge of the Curriculum

To assist pupils to achieve as well as possible in the school setting, attempts need to be made to identify effective schools. This is indeed difficult. Wallberg (1979) identified more than 2,700 research studies that emphasized effective schools. Squires, Huitt, and Segar (1985) in summarizing research pertaining to effective schools raised the following questions:

1. Does the school leader have purpose in mind when administering and supervising in the school setting?
2. Are high academic standards being stressed?

3. Is the principal supportive of efforts in school improvement?
4. Are adequate staff development programmes in evidence to improve the curriculum?
5. Do faculty and staff work together to harmonize endeavours in instructional improvement and discipline of learners.
6. Is the principal visible to observe teaching and learning as well as to confer with teachers on curriculum and instruction matters?

Questions arise here as to what is meant by school and curriculum improvement, having purpose in mind in making changes in the educational setting, as well as which inservice education programmes to stress for faculty development. A need exists to make decisions based on theory. Something must provide direction and guidance in whatever is done in education, teaching, and learning. Writers frequently write about the necessity of theory guiding instruction. These writers tend not to state which theories should be emphasized in the curriculum. There are numerous recommendable psychologies and theories of instruction that can be emphasized in the school curriculum. We recommend strongly that all administrators, supervisors, and teachers become thoroughly familiar with each theory. Depth learning of each theory should be in the offing for educational leaders which includes classroom teachers. These theories have stood the test of time and tend to be classical in nature. We will discuss what we believe to be selected relevant theories of instruction which educational leaders must be able to implement in ongoing lessons and units of study.

Theories of Teaching

Dewey (1916) emphasized *problem solving* approaches in teaching-learning situations. The problems need to be real lifelike to pupils. Committee work to identify and solve contextual problems in a creative atmosphere was stressed.

The teacher is a guide and resource person, not a dispenser of information.

In a science unit on "Animals Without Backbones", pupils individually or in a committee setting might identify problems such as the following based on ongoing learning opportunities:

1. How do sponges obtain food since they do not move around?
2. How do coelenterates, such as jelly fish and the Portuguese man-of-war, paralyze their prey?
3. How do parasites such as flatworms (platyhelminthes) obtain energy for living?

For each problem area identified, pupils may volunteer to serve on a committee to obtain solutions. A variety of reference sources need to be used to gather information in answer to the problem. The answer(s), which are stated as hypotheses, are tentative and subject to testing.

Piaget (1950) stressed a *developmental psychology* by identifying four stages that most pupils go through as they progress from birth through the elementary school years. These developmental stages are sensorimotor (birth to two years of age), preoperational (ages two to seven), concrete operations (ages seven to eleven), and the stage of formal operations (age eleven and beyond). The ages given are approximate in Piaget's research findings.

For the sensorimotor stage of development, which is prior to the public school years, parents may provide models of animals without backbones. These young children may touch, feel, smell, see, and hear sounds of these models when they are being shaken.

At the preoperational stage of development, pupils may raise questions about the invertebrates being observed. Piaget, like Dewey, was strong on using problem solving methods of learning. At this stage of development, Piaget believed that pupils see one variable only or largely such as the length of the object only, or the width only. Comparisons may be too difficult for these preoperational pupils to make such as comparing annelids with platyhelminthes (flatworms) and nematodes (roundworms).

In viewing a videotape, preoperational pupils on the first grade level may notice and reflect upon annelids, such as the earthworm, having a segmented body, and a well developed nervous system. It then might not work for preoperational pupils to make comparisons among invertebrates. The pupils at the stage of concrete operations understand several variables at one time and yet the teacher needs to refer pupils to the concrete situation which are directly related to the abstract. Thus if pupils are studying mollusks, they need to relate abstract learnings (words, phrases, sentences, paragraphs, and diagrams) to the model or real mollusks, including snails, slugs, oysters, and squids. From the concrete to the abstract would be a good model to follow here. Much use needs to be made of real objects and items in teaching pupils on the concrete stage of operations.

At the stage of formal operations, pupils with teacher guidance may discuss arthropods, for example, without referring to realia or concrete situations, according to Piaget. We would recommend, however, that learning activities should stress the concrete facets adequately. Content can become too abstract whereby learners individually do not understand what has been taught.

Marlow (1954) emphasized a theory of motivation with its *hierarchy of needs* that individuals should have fulfilled such as physiological (adequate nutritious food, clothing, and shelter); safety and security (a safe home and neighbourhood, freedom from abuse), love and belonging (acceptance in the home and school setting), esteem (being recognized for talent and/or kill), and self actualization (becoming the kind of person desired). Personal needs of pupils must be met if they are to do well in school. *Pupil—teacher planning* of the curriculum is salient. The objectives, learning opportunities, and appraisal procedures must meet needs of pupils in the science curriculum.

Bruner (1968) emphasized a *structure of knowledge* be identified for each curriculum areas. These structural ideas represent key ideas or major generalizations as perceived by academicians in science in their respective areas of expertise. Leaders in science education and teachers might well identify their own structure of knowledge to emphasize in teaching each curriculum area. Bruner's theory of instruction is practical since its implementation might well provide objectives, learning opportunities to attain the objectives, as well as evaluation procedures to ascertain learner progress. Methods of learning, according to Bruner, emphasize what the scientist would stress in a laboratory setting.

Behaviourism, as a psychology of learning, has a long history of importance (Bobbitt 1916, W.W. Charters 1923, B.F. Skinner 1979). Behaviourism stresses the importance of *precise, measurably stated objectives* for pupil attainment, written prior to instruction. Mastery learning, instructional management systems, and criterion referenced testing are present day examples of behaviourism. Reinforcement theory is also directly relate to behaviourism. The following are examples of behaviourally stated objectives for pupils to achieve:

1. The pupil will list in writing three regions of an insect and explain the purpose of each region.
2. The pupil will write a fifty word paragraph on differences between monerans and bacteria.
3. The pupil will state orally three differences and three likenesses of amphibians versus reptiles.

The science teacher may announce prior to instruction what pupils are to learn from a teaching/learning situation. This provides security to pupils when they know what is to be learned from an ongoing lesson or unit of study. Tests given are aligned with the precisely stated objectives. To provide reinforcement, based on test results, the science teacher may offer sincere praise to pupils for doing well. Ideally, the success rate for pupil learning is high since the teacher teaches directly for pupils achieving the stated objectives. The learning activities aligned with the objectives of instruction make for high validity. With objectives being stated so that pupils either do or do not attain success as a result of interacting with learning opportunities, little leeway is left for interpretation as to what any one objective means.

The *basics* (Bagley, 1905; Bestor, 1953; Smith, 1959) in the curriculum also had a relatively long history in education. It has never been determined at any age in time what is basic for pupils to learn. Former President of the United States Ronald Reagan and his Secretary of Education William Bennett continually emphasized that teachers should teach the basics and not waste time on the frivolous. They too did not define what the basics were that pupils should acquire. If we only could know what these are, much time would be saved in teaching learners. To be sure, effort must always be put forth to determine what is basic and essential for pupils to achieve.

More is expected administrators and supervisors than ever before. Knowledge of the curriculum is no exception. Missouri since 1985 with the Excellence in Education Act, among other states in the United States, mandates that principals evaluate each nontenured teacher at least once a year and tenured teachers at least once every three years. This means that principals need to have knowledge of the curriculum when appraising teaching performance. Teachers will grasp how knowledgeable the principal is during an observation to the classroom followed with a conference. The purpose of observational visits and follow-up conferences should be to improve the teaching of knowledge, skills, and attitudes of the classroom teacher.

Theories of learning to provide direction in teaching-learning situations differ from each other. What then can be done to assist teachers and administrators/supervisors in providing for optimal pupil attainment in the classroom? Determine which theory or theories benefit individual learners in teaching and learning. Pupils differ much from each other and need guidance to learn as much as possible. Since pupils are human beings and are different one from the other, it behooves educational leaders to determine which theory in use will assist the pupil to attain as optimally as possible.

Functions of the Educational Leader

Leaders in education must emphasize the importance of good human and public relations (Shoemaker and Fraser 1981). Principals and supervisors need to assist teachers to have pupils achieve goals. Assisting teachers can largely be done if their is mutual respect and acceptance between the leaders and the teachers. Hindrance in quality communication among participants results in a lack of sharing ideas, results and work completion in the school setting. Oliva (1984) stresses careful attention be given to methods of nonverbal, written, and verbal communication skills.

Gestures, facial expressions, and body movements do convey something to the receiver of nonverbal communication. A friendly conuntenance emphasizing a willingness to work together and collaborate on salient tasks to improve the science curriculum are musts. People realize rather quickly in most cases in which selected individuals indicate nonverbally that they do not wish to serve on a committee, nor give the time to do so, nor indicate feelings of cooperation in moving toward an ideal or have a vision of what should be accomplished in the school setting. The educational leader must present a role model here. The principal/supervisor sets examples for teachers to follow. His/her enthusiasm, knowledge, empathy, and understanding of teachers as human beings having much worth should be an inherent facet of the nonverbal role model. Written communication skills are further needed by the educational leader to convey, clarify, and confirm meaningful information to teachers be it in a bulletin, E-mail, or Fax pertaining notices of staff development, in trends in teaching for teachers to think about, as well as issues in the curriculum. Modern technology has made it so that word processors make the act of written communication easier, neater in the final copy, and more flexible in making revisions and modifications. Mechanical errors must be omitted in all written messages used to communicate to receivers of the message.

Verbal communication must be comprehensible with appropriate stress, pitch, and juncture used to convey information to others. Quality eye contact is a must in verbal communication. Ellis (1986) wrote that, in terms of research results from the studies of William Rutherford and associates, the most successful principals clearly communicated expectations, provided technical assistance, and monitored the results.

Being able to communicate well comes up again and again in research results pertaining to educational leaders. Hallinger and Murphy (1986) in emphasizing effective school research summaries list the following as being salient:

1. determining and communicating the goals of the school;
2. supervising and evaluating teaching and learning;
3. coordinating curriculum efforts;
4. developing high standards in the academics as well as high expectations;
5. monitoring and evaluating student achievement;
6. encouraging professional development of teachers;
7. maintaining time on task for instruction;
8. developing incentives for teachers and students.

Stocklinski and Miller—Colbert (1991) emphasize the Comer Process, a research based model for school improvement that has as its basis collaboration, consensus, and communication for the solving of problems in academic, social and staff development areas. This process permits teachers, supervisors/principals, and parents to harmonize efforts in working together for the good of the pupil. Among other items of importance here is the emphasis placed upon quality *communication* to achieve goals of the school and of education.

Traits and Characteristics of Principals

More is expected in a complex society than ever before of school supervisors and administrators

Duttweiler and Hord (1989) state that educational leaders who are effective desire a participatory style of supervision.

These principals and supervisors want input from others, particularly teachers. Thus there needs to be collaboration skills in working together for the good of the student. Skills in being able to foster cooperation among participants in selecting objectives of instruction, learning opportunities to attain the objectives, and evaluation procedures to assess progress are desired from school leaders. These leaders need to be able to motivate, encourage, and stimulate others in the school setting to participate in school improvement endeavours. Thus principals and supervisors should be skillful in working effectively with others to achieve the goals of the school. An open school environment assists participants to become actively involved to improve the total school curriculum.

Society is continually changing. It does not stay stable. With the many societal changes, the school curriculum also needs modification and revisions. The world of work and the personal needs of individuals require that student competencies need developing in the areas of creative thing, problems solving, critical thinking, as well as reasoning skills (Dede 1989). Educational leaders should think of change as being relevant in society. These changes have tremendous implications for objectives and goals in the curriculum, learning opportunities to attain the stated ends, and assessment procedures to determine how much pupils have learned and what is left to be done to guide more optimal learner attainment.

The new leader in the school setting must be

1. highly knowledgeable of workable procedures of teaching;
2. an effective leader possessing skills to work with others;
3. able to motivate teachers and others in the school setting;
4. proficient in curriculum development;
5. knowledge of child development characteristics;
6. proficient in a variety of communication skills;

7. skillful in interpersonal relations;
8. able to plan and implement decisions made through collaboration;
9. knowledge of societal trends and quality school practices;
10. able to apply technology to instruction and management;
11. skillful in the use of political processes to attain objectives of instruction;
12. knowledge about school site management and its implication;
13. secure parental cooperation and input;
14. obtain information to use in making relevant decisions;
15. empower individuals, especially teachers, in a rich school cultural climate.

School leaders need to provide opportunities for science teachers to try out new ideas in ongoing lessons and units of study. Thus, science teachers with supervisor leadership may wish to assist pupils in new ways to develop rich science vocabularies. Condrey (1996) wrote the following:

Every science teacher knows that showing students how concepts apply to everyday events is quite a challenge. We describe real world application in class, conduct demonstrations to illustrate concepts in action, and give students applications they can replicate in the lab. Yet they still have difficulty connecting classroom activities to their own lives.

We could spend hours previewing videos in search of the perfect visual to illustrate concepts germane to teenagers' lives. A better idea is to provide them the opportunity to produce a video that illustrates concept applications from their own experiences.

Student teams can design and produce three to five minute instructional videos that define a concept and apply it to their personal experiences. For example, physics students might film applications of inertia in skating or stock car racing: biology or anatomy students might show how a gymnast's muscles work together to perform a manoeuvre on the parallel bars; or chemistry students might produce a video illustrating the effects of chemical reactions in food preparation. Making these videos helps students to see the connections between science and 'real life' by taking the experience out of the classroom and putting it into their personal areas of knowledge and relevance.

Producing a short video involves much more than haphazard filming. The purpose is to define and illustrate the application of a specific concept, so the video should be instructive and follow a logical sequence. It must be able to stand alone without further explanations from the presenters. Students should be encouraged to use creativity and humor in their productions.

In Summary

Foresight of educational leaders is vital so that a vision of the ideal is possible. Efforts need to be made to achieve the vision. It is an ongoing process. Much knowledge of the curriculum is necessary to attain and grow. Purposes need to be involved in moving from what is to what should be. The educational leader needs to provide support to those working toward positive changes in curriculum improvement. Staff development is needed in making these changes. Collaboration among participants is necessary to work toward a desired curriculum.

Diverse theories of instruction that have stood the test of time may be used by teachers to guide pupils to achieve as much as possible. The theory used must harmonize with what assists the learner(s) to attain and achieve. Each theory provides the teacher guidance and direction in making educational decisions.

Quality supervisors/principals are able to communicate well with others. Diverse forms of communication must be used to achieve purposes in the school setting. The goals and objectives of the school need communicating to parents and the lay public. Learning opportunities being emphasized in the school setting should harmonize with quality goals and objectives. Monitoring of learner progress in goal attainment is a must. These need to be high standards for pupil achievement with time on task involved. Incentives for learning and for teaching should be in the offing.

Society changes rather continuously making it necessary for the school curriculum to change. Higher levels of cognition must be stressed in teaching-learning situations. Knowledgeable, skillful leaders should possess abilities to work effectively with others, especially teachers. These leaders must be proficient in curriculum development procedures. Child growth and development characteristics should be used in improving teaching and learning. Good interpersonal relations are needed to guide staff development efforts as well as involve parents in matters pertaining to curriculum improvement.

There are principles of learning from educational psychology which teachers and educational leaders tend to agree with. These principles of learning provide guidance in choosing objectives of instruction, learning opportunities for pupils to achieve the objectives, as well as appraisal procedures to ascertain what pupils have learned. Ediger (1994) lists these principles of learning as follows:

1. pupils need to attach meaning and understanding to ongoing lessons and units of study;
2. pupils need to experience interest in learning;
3. pupils need to perceive purpose in learning;
4. pupils need to experience sequence in learning opportunities;
5. pupils need to experience rational balance among objectives in the curriculum, such as knowledge, skills and attitudinal goals.

The long range goal of educational leaders is to assist teachers in guiding pupils to achieve more optimally. Supervisors/principals need to challenge teachers to provide the best curriculum possible for pupils in the school setting.

Ward, *et. al.* (1996) wrote the following:

> As students continue to explore the observations and relationships found in the above activities, the teacher guides students to 'construct' the concept that air expands when heated and contracts when cooled. The teacher then provides opportunities for pupils to apply that concept to new situations in which differences in air pressure are caused by the temperature changes.

Providing a classroom environment that encourages collaborations among students is an important component of a constructivist classroom environment. When teachers use questions that probe, clarify, and explore the relationships between student's prior experiences, students develop more accurate science concepts.

Students within this classroom environment change from passive receptors to active learners responsible for their own construction of meaning. The challenge for teachers is how to help students effectively construct meaning. Teachers continued to be responsible for selecting which science concepts to study and how their students learn these concepts. Within a constructivist environment, however, these decisions are based to a much larger degree on the abilities of teachers to know what their students bring to the classroom. When teachers are attuned to students' prior knowledge, they enable students to accommodate their previously held 'understandings' by providing experiences that develop increased understanding of science concepts.

REFERENCES

Richardson, M.D., and others. "A Descriptive Analysis of Kentucky Elementary School Principals." ERIC Document Reproduction Service ED 311557.

Ediger, Marlow, "Goals of School Administrators," *Michigan Principal*, Fall, 1993, pp 12-14.

Walberg, H., and others. "The Quiet Revolution in Education Research," *Phi Delta Kappan*, November, 1979, pp 179-183.

Squires, David, and others. *Effective Schools and Classrooms: A Research Based Perspective*. Alexandria, Virginia: Association for Supervision and Curriculum Development, 1985.

Dewey, John, *Democracy and Education*. New York: The Macmillan Company, 1916.

Piaget, Jean, *The Psychology of Intelligence*. New York: Harcourt Brace Jovanovich, 1950.

Bruner, Jerome, *Toward a Theory of Instruction*. Cambridge, Massachusetts: Harvard University Press, 1968.

Bobbitt, Franklin, *The Curriculum*. Boston: Houghton Mifflin Company, 1918.

Charters, W.W. Charters, *Curriculum Construction*. New York: The Macmillan Company, 1923.

Skinner, B.F., *Beyond Freedom and Dignity*. New York: Alfred Knopf, Inc. 1979.

Bagley, William, *The Educative Process*. New York: The Macmillan Company, 1905.

Bestor, Arthur, *Educational Wastelands*. Urbana: University of Illinois Press, 1953.

Smith, Mortimer, *Diminished Mind*. Chicago: Regency Press, 1959.

Shoemaker, J., and Fraser, H.W "What Principals Can Do: Some Implications from Studies of Effective Schooling," *Phi Delta Kappan*. November, 1981, pp. 178-182.

Oliva, P.F., *Supervision for Today's Schools*. New York: Longman, 1984.

Ellis, T.I., "The Principal as Instructional Leader." ERIC Document Reproduction Service. ED 274301, 1986.

Hallinger, P., and J. Murphy. "Instructional Leadership in Effective Schools." ERIC Document Reproduction Service ED 309535, 1986.

Stocklinski, J., and J. Miller-Colbert, "The Comer Process Moving from I to We." ERIC Document Reproductive Service EJ 419920 1986.

Duttwelier, F.C., and S. Hord. *Dimensions of Effective School Leadership*. Austin, Texas: BEDL, 1989.

Dede, C., "The Evolution of Information Technology: Implications for Curriculum," *Educational Leadership*, Volume 47(1), 23-26.

National Association of Elementary School Principals, *Principals for the Twenty First Century Schools*. Alexandria, Virginia: NAESP, 1990.

Ediger, Marlow, "Early Field Experiences in Teacher Education," College Student Journal, September, 1994, pp 302-307.

Ward, Kathleen, *et. al*. (1996), Constructing Scientific Knowledge, *The Science Teacher*, 63 (9), 23.

Condrey, Jean Friend (1996). Focus on Science Concepts, *The Science Teacher* 63 (4), 17.

5

Staff Development Programmes in Science

Much is written in educational literature pertaining to staff development. It appears that writers stress staff development for each innovation presented. For example, if the interdisciplinary curriculum needs emphasis, then staff development is needed. Or, if full inclusion is wanted, then staff development should be in evidence. We believe the first issue in staff development is how many sessions should be devoted to staff development when writers bring in new ideas in teaching and at the same time advocate staff development for implementing that idea. Is it necessary to have staff development for each new or innovative idea adopted in teaching and learning? Might teachers be trusted with implementing the new concept(s) on their own?

Further Issues in Staff Development

Who should determine what should be emphasized in staff development? A common vision is being emphasized as to what our schools should be like as a result of this vision. How is the vision to be achieved? A staff development programme, in part, may help. Ediger (1988) recommends that staff development programmes have three integrated parts such as a general session, small group or committee endeavours, and individual study. Teachers here should determine what is to be emphasized in the general session to identify problem areas, they should volunteer as to which committee to work on to solve problems, and then work individually on a problem of their very own choosing. The teacher and teaching here are at the centre of the stage in staff development. Principals and supervisors are there to assist teachers in working toward solutions of problem areas.

Toward the other end of the continuum, supervisors and principals, after consultation with teachers, may desire to bring in a certain programme whereby staff development is necessary. The teachers are trained and educated to use a certain model in teaching after a quality programme of training. This approach at staff development has unique features that the first did not possess. The latter procedure in staff development is more principal/supervisor oriented, even though there was consultation with teachers about the new approach. Second, a commercial approach or one proposed by a team of educators was emphasized. The ideas for problem areas to be solved basically did not come from local teachers. Third, teachers must develop into having completely new teaching styles. The teaching model selected for staff development and implementation might not intrinsically be wanted by teachers. There may be a different procedure in teaching desired by teachers. Fourth, an external training team may be involved in the training of teachers. Trainers then come from outside the local school system or district. Fifth, trainers sequence experiences for teachers in staff training sessions. A logical approach is then involved in sequencing experiences for trainees.

What Should Training Sessions Stress?

The objectives of instruction may be changed or modified. Generally cognitive objectives have received major emphasis in the curriculum. There are different levels of pupils achievement in the cognitive domain. Changes may be made from stressing the lower level cognitive objectives to those emphasizing higher levels of thinking. Bloom's (1956) is still popular in discussing objectives from the lower to higher levels of cognition. His sequence is the following: recall of factual information by learners, comprehension of what has been recalled, application or using what has been learned, analysis involving critical thought, synthesis stressing unique ways of putting the information together after analysis, and evaluation of what has been learned in terms of standards or criteria. Staff development programmes may stress teachers having children move for lower to higher cognitive objectives using Bloom's taxonomy. Learning opportunities need to be designed to guide pupils in thinking at a more complex level in ongoing learning opportunities. Feedback from teachers to members of the staff development programme should be in the offing after the teacher has used higher cognitive objectives in the classroom.

There is much discussion in education about having pupils apply what has been learned. Perhaps, a staff development programme will stress the level of application in ongoing training sessions. Teachers then put to use ideas developed and acquired in the staff development programme to the regular classroom. These teachers report back to the training session how the ideas worked out in the classroom.

Modification of objectives stressed in teaching and learning may also emphasize minimizing cognitive and advocating affective ends in teaching. Affective objectives put more emphasis upon attitudes that pupils need to develop. Hopefully, quality attitudes will assist pupils to achieve cognitive objectives more effectively. Krathwohl stressed five levels of affective objectives in moving from the lowest to the higher levels. These are the following: paying attention to relevant content presented, responding to content with feeling or emotion, responding to content in a value oriented way, organising values and feelings into a structure, and characterizing the attitudes in terms of being consistent and following a pattern. A quality affective curriculum emphasizes pupils developing positive feelings and values.

A learning stations philosophy might well stress an affective curriculum. Here, the teacher together with pupils develop an adequate number of stations as well as tasks for each station. Pupils might then choose which tasks to complete and which to omit. Decision-making by learners is important. Ideally, pupils choose tasks which possess interest and perceived purpose. Motivation for learning should be higher if the pupil has had input into what he/she has planned and wishes to learn. The learner also is involved in planning and selecting—two concepts which no doubt are at the heart of democratic thinking. The learner chooses from among alternatives and he/she is affected by choices made, from among alternatives. Involvement by pupils in selecting objectives, learning activities, and appraisal procedures emphasizes increasingly democratic living. Also the attitudes of the pupil determine, in part, what will be learned. A psychological curriculum stresses pupils sequencing their very own learning opportunities; opposite of a psychological curriculum is a logical curriculum whereby a teacher arranges the order of learning for pupils.

In noticing that an almost complete absence of statement advocating democracy and democratic ideals from policy makers. Fenstermacher (1995) write the following:

...We hear a great deal about readying the next generation of workers for global competition, about being first in the world in such high status subjects as math and science, and about having world class standards for what is learned in school. We hear almost nothing about civic participation or building and maintaining democratic communities, whether these be neighbourhoods or governments at the local, state or federal levels. The advancement of democratic ideals and institutions goes largely unmentioned, taken for granted or insufficiently important to rank up there with such world—shaking events as our playing Avis to Japan's Hertz.

Workshops and staff development programmes might then be arranged for the teacher to stress democracy as a way of life with the inclusion of affective objectives.

A third change in the curriculum may reflect the use of psychomotor objectives. Here, the school curriculum stresses the use of the gross and finer muscles of the learner. Horrow (1972) listed six levels of psychomotor objectives. These are the following:

1. reflex movement;
2. basic fundamental movements, including locomotor, non-locomotor manipulative movements;
3. perceptual abilities containing several subcategories;
   (a) kinesthetic discrimination that refers to body awareness, body image, body relationship of surrounding objects in space;
   (b) visual discrimination including visual awareness, visual tracking, visual memory, figure ground differentiation, and perceptual constancy;
   (c) auditory discrimination including auditory activity; tracking and memory;
   (d) tactile discrimination;
   (e) coordination.
4. physical abilities including endurance, strength, flexibility, and agility;
5. skilled movement including simple adaptive skill, compound and complex adaptive skill;
6. non-discursive communication including expressive movements and interpretive movements.

In emphasizing psychomotor objectives, the teacher assists pupils to become actively involved in making, constructing, artistic endeavours, doing, and other forms of using physical movement and motion. Psychomotor objectives may be used in any curriculum area and receive more emphasis in teaching and learning as compared to cognitive and affective ends of instruction (Earnest, 1995).

Staff development programmes may be needed to change from a cognitive or affective objective emphasis to one stressing the psychomotor domain. Psychomotor objectives truly emphasize an activity centred curriculum for pupils. I supervise student teachers and regular teachers in the public school setting. In teaching a unit on "Weather and How It Affects Us," pupils with teaching team guidance discussed and constructed a barometer, a wind vane, a hygrometer, and an anemometer. Each object was goal centred, planned, constructed, and appraised in terms of criteria.

Learning Opportunities to Achieve Objectives

In changing from previously used activities and experiences to a new approach takes effort, knowledge, skill and motivation. If pupils are to use modern technology in the curriculum, it may truly revolutionize the curriculum depending upon the amount of change being emphathized. In using the word processor, world wide web and internet, graphing techniques, CD ROMS, video disks, among other items, teachers may need to experience two to three years of quality staff development programmes. Objectives need to be determined for pupils to achieve sequentially in using modern technology. Progress by pupils may well be slow, but sure with good teaching, in using technology to achieve objectives.

Second, staff development programmes might well be extensive if an interdisciplinary curriculum is to be in evidence. An allied arts programme of instruction may well emphasize a team teaching approach. Allied arts attempts to integrate art, music, dance, drama, poetry, and architecture, among other possibilities. Thus a teaching team consisting of the following teachers, each qualified in his/her area of expertise—an art, a music, a physical education, and a literature or English teacher—must be in the offing. If possible, an architecture from the community might be hired part time. If the school system has an architect, it becomes easier for this person to work on the team to plan the objectives, learning opportunities, and evaluation procedures than would otherwise be the case. Staff development programmes might then include members learning to plan together, developing means of curricular integration of content, and evaluating to ascertain the effectiveness of the teaching team. Team teaching has built-in in-service education opportunities since members may learn from each other during planning sessions.

Third, cooperative learning, as activities and experiences for pupils to achieve objectives, may need staff development programmes. The goals of the staff development programme might stress how to form groups for cooperative learning, how to work effectively as a teacher with diverse groups in the classroom, and how to appraise pupil performance within a group. The classroom teacher needs to believe in cooperative learning for it to become effective in the classroom setting.

There needs to be a caring attitude toward each other in cooperative learning endeavours. Pupils who feel neutral to each other or possess feelings of hostility might well fail to become good members of a committee in cooperative learning endeavours. Noddings (1995) wrote the following:

> The greatest structural obstacle, however, may be simply legitimizing the inclusion of themes of care in the curriculum. Teachers in the early grades have long included such themes as a regular part of their work, and middle school educators are becoming more sensitive to developmental needs involving care. But, secondary schools—where violence, apathy, and alienation are most evident—do little to develop the capacity to care. Today, even elementary teachers complain that the pressure to produce high test scores inhibit the work they believe is central to their mission: the development of competent and caring people. Therefore it would seem that the most fundamental change required is one of attitude. Teachers can be very special people in the lives of children, and it should be legitimate for them to spend time developing relations to trust, talking with students about problems that are central to their lives, and guiding them toward greater sensitivity and competence across all the domains of care.

Fourth, peer coaching may be used to assist teachers to hone and perfect teaching skills in any curriculum area. Two teachers working together may observe each other's teaching and discuss the quality of objectives to be stressed, the aligning of learning opportunities with the objectives, and evaluation to ascertain if the objectives have been achieved by pupils. Showers and Joyce (1996), strong advocates of peer coaching, wrote the following:

> When staff development becomes the major vehicle for school improvement, schools should take into account both the structures and content of training, as well as changes needed in the workplace to make possible the collaborative planning, decision making, and data collection that are essential to organisational change efforts. As we ponder ways to ensure that training/coaching fuels the school renewal process, we are also examining how the culture of the school can increasingly provide a benign environment for collective activity.
>
> A cohesive school culture makes possible the collective decisions that generate schoolwide improvement efforts. The formation of peer coaching teams produce greater faculty cohesion and focus and, in turn, facilitates more skillful shared decision making. A skillful staff development programme results in a self-perpetuating process for change as well as new knowledge and skills for teachers and increased learning for pupils.

Peer coaching might then be used to improve the quality of learning opportunities for pupils as well as select objectives and evaluation procedures for learners. Learning opportunities (Ediger, 1994) should emphasize that pupils experience

1. meaningful lessons and units of study. With meaning, pupils understand and comprehend that which was contained in ongoing learning opportunities;
2. interesting content and skills in the curriculum. With interest, the pupil and the curriculum become one, not separate entities. Pupils attend and achieve from ongoing lessons and units of study;

3. purpose in learning. With purpose in learning, pupils accept reasons for attaining relevant facts, concepts, and generalizations presented...;
4. sequence in learning, with quality sequence, pupils relate newly acquired content with that previously achieved. Previous knowledge attained provides readiness for the new objectives to be achieved...;
5. balance among objectives stressed. Thus, knowledge, skills, and attitudes—three kinds of objectives need to be achieved by students. These objectives interact and are not in isolation from each other. For example, if pupils possess positive attitudes, they should achieve needed knowledge and skills more readily.

Traditional organisation of learning opportunities stress using textbooks heavily, workbooks, work sheets, and recitation methods of instruction. A separate subjects curriculum tends to be in evidence with traditional approaches in teaching. Moving away from the separate subjects curriculum is correlation, then fusion, and finally the interdisciplinary curriculum. Skill in planning is needed to move away from the usual ways of teaching to that which harmonizes more so with learner growth and development characteristics. Each pupil is to realize optimal development in knowledge, skills, and attitudes or the affective dimension. A multimedia approach is recommended in teaching to provide for individual differences.

Evaluation of Pupil Progress

Traditional procedures of evaluating pupil achievement has been to use standardized and norm referenced testing. Teacher written test items have also been used much in the past to ascertain pupil progress. These procedures are still recommended to determine pupil achievement. However, addition procedures must be used. Teacher observation needs to be used to notice learner progress in contextual situations. Thus within a given activity, the teacher notices how well each pupil is progressing. Assistance is given to pupils as is necessary. Pupils might then continue to work in context on the project or activity being pursued.

A relatively recent development is for pupils with teacher guidance to develop a portfolio of achievement and progress. In the portfolio, the pupil places samples of activities completed. These include written work, art projects, snapshots of construction experiences, videotapes of dramatic endeavours, and cassette recordings of speech activates among others. The portfolio may also contain test results, journal entries, rating scales, rubrics, and checklists to indicate learner progress and achievement. Materials for the portfolio must be carefully chosen; otherwise it may become too voluminous. Contents in the portfolio are to show interested persons accomplishments of the involved pupil. A variety of learning opportunities experienced by a learner must show its related accomplishments to others who are interested in seeing the individual pupil's achievements.

Kane and Khattri (1995) wrote:

Some questions related to performance assessment remain to be answered by future research. They have to do with basic and secondary issues in educational reform. What knowledge and skills are students expected to demonstrate after a certain period of schooling? What other systematic reforms must be undertaken in order for assessment reforms to be effective? Which assessment formats are most useful for which specific purposes? The greatest challenge ahead lies in designing systems of school reform that synergistically support the core educational functions of teaching and learning for which teachers are the most powerful 'engine'.

REFERENCES

Bloom, Benjamin S. (1956). *Taxonomy of Educational Objectives, Handbook One—Cognitive Domain*. London, England: Longmans Publishing House.

Earnest Vimala (1995). *The Relative Effectiveness of Teaching Volumetric Experiments in Chemistry Using Simpson's Taxonomy of Educational Objectives for the Psychomotor Domain—An Experimental Study*, Ph.D. Thesis. University of Madras, India, pp. 4-21.

Ediger, Marlow (1988). *The Elementary Curriculum*, 2nd Edition, Kirksville, Missouri: Simpson Publishing Company, pp. 117-126.

Ediger, Marlow (1994). "Early Field Experiences in Teacher Education," *College Student Journal*, 28: 302.

Ediger, Marlow and Digumarti Bhaskara Rao (2003). *Elementary Curriculum*. New Delhi: Discovery Publishing House.

Fenstermacher, Gary D. (1995). "The Absence of Democratic and Educational Ideals from Contemporary Educational Reforms Initiatives," *Educational Horizons,* 73: 70.

Kene, Michael B., and Nidh Khattri (1995). "Assessment Reform," the *Phi Delta Kappan*, 77: 32.

Krathwohl, David, *et al*. (1956). *The Taxonomy of Educational Objectives. Handbook Two, Affective Domain*. London, England: Longmans Publishing House.

Noddings, Neil (1995). "Teaching Themes of Care," *Phi Delta Kappan*. 76: 679.

Showers, Beverly, and Bruce Joyce (1996). "The Evolution of Peer Coaching," *Educational Leadership*, 53: 16.

6

Technology in Elementary Science

There is strong emphasis placed upon use of modern technology in the elementary school curriculum. Technology is very strongly used in all facets of society, and elementary schools should not lag behind what is stressed in the societal arena. The elementary pupil of today will be expected to achieve in a heavily endowed work place involving technology. Many factories and farms have been strongly automated. Fewer workers are continually needed in these works places. Machines automatically do work that was formally done with the use of human muscles and physical work.

Generally, people think of farming as stressing that very heavy manual labour is done continuously. Egg production, as one example, has eliminated most of the manual labour that was formerly done. As a high school student working at home after school hours and in summer, I pumped water by hand and carried it to the hen house, approximately seventy yards from the hand operated water pump. I carried buckets of feed from the barn to the laying house and put it in a feeder for the laying hens. I gathered eggs from the nests by placing the eggs in a bucket. The bucket became very heavy when gathering more and more eggs. Cleaning the hen house was indeed an undesirable chore. Presently with six hens in a cage and the cages being placed in rows, one person can take care of 15,000 laying hens readily, whereas I took care of 300 hens with a lot of manual labour involved. Today, the eggs fall down from the cages, onto a conveyor belt. A person at the end of the long row presses a button and all the eggs come down to where this worker is located. A machine is even available to pack the eggs into a create. The feed goes down a conveyer belt every fifty minutes so that the laying hens have plenty to eat in order to produce eggs. The feed is augurred automatically from a bin outside the laying house. Water also goes down the troughs continually for laying hens to drink. A truck comes to pick up the crates of eggs two times a week. The owner largely manages the laying house operation to see that all machines are working properly. Not all farm work, by any means is automated to this extent. In contrast, any person who has cut, baled, and hauled hay realizes the heavy use of muscles that are presently involved here.

At a cigarette factory, everything is automated including quality control. In other words, when the cigarettes have been packaged, the machine will cull out what was not done properly. Workers are there, few in number, to notice when involved machines are not working properly. They are then responsible for repair work when needed or to obtain assistance if someone else needs to do the work.

Menial work that requires human feats pays very little money, but even here the manual labour done by a human being is rather minimal, such as in fast food restaurants. At these fast food restaurants, there is a lot of movement and motion by workers in getting fast food orders fulfilled. No doubt, these workers get tired after being at the task, but the labour is not intensive.

When on a farm, as mentioned above, farmers would shovel wheat by hand, since grain augers had not yet been perfected adequately. Shovelling grain by hand with a scoop is labour intensive. They became tired after shovelling fifty bushels of wheat from a pickup into a grain bin: there were many fifty bushel loads that needed shovelling in one day during harvest time. The grain auger took most of the human efforts out of shovelling wheat since the wheat was now augurred rapidly, fifty bushels in three minutes, using an attached electric motor to the auger. What does this discussion have to do with the use of modern technology in the elementary school classroom?

Personal Beliefs About Technology Use

There are selected criteria from the psychology of learning that need emphasis in having pupils work with technology. We believe that technology should capture pupil interests in learning. Activities here should be fascinating to engage pupil interaction. These interests should provide for effort in pupils desiring to achieve, grow and develop. There is little time for misbehaviour if pupils are interested in the task at hand. We have noticed, for example, first graders who had little interest in drill and practice in arithmetic using paper and pencil. And yet when a hand held calculator or computer programme was emphasized, these learners truly showed interest and fascination in learning. Interest is a powerful factor in learning since attention to the task at hand makes for increased achievement.

Second, we believe that technology may assist learners to perceive purpose in learning. If purpose is lacking, there will be little incentive for pupils to learn. Goal centred pupils achieve more than those who fail to perceive objectives in learning. We have observed many pupils who did not like to check long division problems using paper and pencil. Again, when the checking was done rapidly and accurately with the calculator or computer, there seemingly was even joy in doing the checking to see if the long division problem had been worked correctly. It appeared that pupils saw purpose, not drudgery, in checking these long division problems.

Third, we believe technology can assist pupils to attach meaning to ongoing lessons and units of study. What pupils learn then should make sense, not be nonsense tasks. There are numerous programmes in computer use which guide pupils to achieve an objective. These numerous ways stress if one procedure is not understood, there are other approaches which will guide pupils to attach meaning. It is so important that pupils understand what is being learned. Many of us have learned that do divide fractions, we need to invert the divisor and then multiply. This mechanical procedure made no sense to me in grade school and in high school. There should be meaning in why 'the divisor is inverted and then multiply." With clear illustrations together with the abstract numerals on the monitor, pupils may well understand and attach meaning as to why to "invert the divisor and multiply." What is learned should make sense and not merely be committed to memory.

Computer programmes should assist pupils to perceive knowledge as being related, not in isolated bits. One of the authors noticed a delightful programme on a monitor with high pupil enthusiasm working on the Egyptian system of numeration when studying a social studies unit on the Middle East. Here, pupils were fascinated to learn that individual strokes represented the numerals from one through nine. Further interests were shown in the following features of the Egyptian system of numeration:

1. each heel bone of an ox, shaped like an arch represented a value of ten. Nine heel bones represented a value of ninety;
2. each coiled rope represented a value of 100. There could be as many as nine coiled ropes to represent a value of 900;
3. each lotus flower represented 1,000. The pattern is that nine lotus flowers represent a value of 9,000;
4. each bent finger represented a value of 10,000. Nine bent fingers represent 90,000;
5. each tadpole represent 100,000, thus nine tadpoles represent 900,000.

We present this information, as an example, to show that computer programmes along with other technologies can definitely assist pupils to perceive that knowledge is related. In this case, social studies and mathematics can definitely be related so that the learner perceives the interrelationship of subject matter. Morris and Pai (1976) wrote the following pertaining to Jerome Bruner's thinking on the relationship of knowledge:

...since human beings seem to be able to store more information than they can spontaneously recall, the main problem in human memory is that of effective retrieval. Bruner is convinced that the key to effective retrieval is organisation of information. He contends there is sufficient evidence to support the assertion that, in general, any information organized around the interests and then cognitive structure of the learner can be most efficiently recalled. Hence, the only means by which we can reduce the quick rate of loss of human memory is to organise facts according the basic principles and concepts from which they were inferred. Further, "the very attitude and activities that also seem to have the effect of conserving characterize figuring out or discovering things for ourself also seem to have the effect of conserving memory." In addition to these effects, the learning experiences resulting from self-discovery give us an increased awareness of the connections and continuities between what we learn and what we do. As a result, we are likely to see our activities in a broader context and thus gain more control of our acts in relation to an end in view. In learning by discovery, knowledge already possessed by the learner is used to gain new insights and, and in the process old knowledge becomes reconstructed.

Being very strong on learning by discovery, Jerome Bruner, stresses organising information around the interests and cognitive structure of pupils. Discovery conserves or saves what has been learned previously. Pupils need to use knowledge to obtain new insights thus connecting what we learn and what we do. There are many key ideas Bruner presents here for learners to relate knowledge and increase memory/recall. The use of technology such as video-tapes and software programmes can and do assist pupils to relate knowledge inductively and thus retain content for a longer duration of time.

Fifth, the use of technology can certainly assist to provide for individual differences among pupils in terms of achievement in diverse academic areas. When pupils work on computer programmes, they can definitely work at their optimal rate of achievement individually. Thus, in a tutorial programme for example, pupils need to possess readiness factors such as having adequate background information. The learner then may move forward on that programme at an as optimal rate as possible. Comparing this learning situation with viewing a video-tape, the contents in the latter may move forward too rapidly or too slowly.

Sixth, technology and its use might well guide pupils to develop wholesome attitudes toward learning. Pupils seem to be fascinated with interacting with technology. We have observed pupils in classrooms with little interest in achieving in mathematics, as an example, until it is time for the learner to work with the computer. Here, the pupil interacted with drawings and abstract related numerals on the monitor. Problem solving was stressed here for a fifth grade pupil emphasizing finding the volume of a cone. The drawings were excellent and the hints given in finding the volume were sequential to permit the learner to determine the needed answer. Later, another pupil also came to the computer to solve additional problems cooperatively. The interest was high and the two learners worked together harmoniously. The joy that comes in working with others truly has its values for pupils.

Philosophy of Education and Technology

We are strong believes in teachers, not only stressing the psychology of learning, but also the philosophy of education in technology use. There are selected philosophies that teachers need to understand and use in teaching-learning situations.

A first philosophy and its use we would like to discuss is experimentalism. Experimentalists believe strongly in a changing environment. Changes occur in all facets of the social/natural environment. Rather rapid changes have occurred such as in technology. When we first started teaching, there were no word processors on our campuses. Typewriters were available. Electric typewriters quickly replaced the manual typewriters. Word processors rapidly replaced the electric typewriters. Changes can and do occur rapidly. There is hardly anything, objects as well as ideas, where change does not occur.

Change is a key concept in experimentalism. With change, new problems arise. These problems need identification and delimitation so that they can be solved. An hypothesis is developed in answer to the problem. The hypothesis is tentative, never an absolute. Each hypothesis is to be tested in a lifelike situation. Problems, hypotheses, and tests of hypotheses are done in context within a practical situation. Experimentalism is utilitarian, not abstract nor theoretical. Pertaining to John Dewey and his beliefs on change, Ediger (1995) wrote the following:

John Dewey (1859-1952) lived during a period of rapid change. When he was born and even until the early 1900s, the automobile basically did not exist. When he died in 1952, manufactured automobiles, as a whole, were very dependable with hydraulic brakes, heaters, and even a few with air conditioners. Electricity had its beginning in home and factory use in the early 1890s and was highly refined with its uses in 1952, with electric ranges, dishwashers, clothes washers, and driers. Changes have occurred from zero automobiles in 1859 to more highways and inter-states being built to take care of the large number of automobiles in use in the present time. In 1859 horse drawn farm equipment was utilized to plow, harrow, disk, and seed the farm land. By 1952 farm tractors had electric lights, hydraulic brakes, and could pull a plow with four to five shears in plowing the land. Tremendous changes then occurred from 1859 (year of birth) to 1952 (year of death of Dr. Dewey).

With these and many other changes, problems arise. Problems need identification and careful delineation in the school curriculum, as well as in society. Each problem is vital. Information acquired in school needs to be utilized to solve problems. Knowledge is not attained for its own sake, but is instrumental to the solving of identified problems. In society also, information is secured from a variety of reference sources, useful to solve each chosen problem.

From the data gathered, directly related to the problem, a hypothesis is developed. A hypothesis results for each identified problem. The hypothesis is tentative and subject to change through testing. Testing is done in a life-like situation. The results of the test may confirm or refute the hypothesis. Minor revisions of the hypothesis may also be needed. Generally, change will occur rather continuously.

Experimentalists believe that one can only know experience. One cannot know the real world in whole or in part as realists advocate nor does one know ideas only, of what exists out there in society, as idealists stress. With the world of experience as experimentalists believe, one identifies and solves necessary problems. Eichelberger (1989) wrote the following pertaining to pragmatism, also called experimentalism.

The relationship between knowledge and reality (truth) that is used by researchers today is that of the pragmatist, which states that all knowledge is produced by human beings and that we can never distinguish between knowledge and truth. In empirical research, this means that if something works in practice then it is true, or we can assume that it is true. A truth (knowledge) that is not supported by further empirical study will be modified or discarded.

How does any philosophy of education relate directly to the use of technology? We have noticed numerous computerized programmes that are excellent for pupils to use in problem solving. Thus pupils in context have identified a problem for which they wish to have or find a solution. A software programme carefully selected might well provide data to test a hypothesis. Generally, additional technological sources will be used to evaluate an identified hypothesis in answer to a problem. However, there are numerous programmes which may provide information in the problem solving arena. Then too, there are simulated programmes which tend to be lifelike and real. These entire software programmes go through flexible steps of problem solving. A delightful computerized simulation is Choice or Chance (1984). This simulated programme

1. relate diverse academic disciplines;
2. brings reality into the curriculum;
3. emphasizes active involvement on the part of learners;
4. presents background information to pupils before decisions are considered and made;
5. involves a logical sequence in that the programmers present sequential problems for pupils to consider;
6. stresses low risk on the pupil's part in interacting since the materials are not first hand, but are reality based.

Changes in technology abound. Rose and Fernland wrote:

During the 1990's, computer assisted instruction (CIA) was an important part of classroom use. Teachers, department chairs, and district technology coordinators purchased commercial and public domain programmes in the subject areas, stored on one or more floppy disks, including drill and practice programmes, tutorials, simulations, and games. During the next decade there were four major changes that improved CAI: *(i)* the decline of the use of floppy disks, replaced by the enhanced storage capability of CD-ROM and videodisc, *(ii)* enhanced interactivity in software in which students play a more active role, *(iii)* sophisticated graphics, video clips, colour and sound, creating a multimedia presentation no longer dominated by screens of text; and *(iv)* the growing marriage of CAI and telecommunications, allowing a seamless transition from single computer use to collaborative work with distant partners and access to internet-based sources.

The use of CAI in the social studies classroom continues to be strong, although such use is being eclipsed by the tool uses of computers; word processing; communications, research, and multimedia production. CAI is available on the internet, a helpful tool for teachers who want to review the product and consult other teachers who have used the programme with their students. CAI has greatly improved in creativity and quality; many programmes offer motivating experiences for students in analysis, problem solving, and decision making.

Idealism as a Philosophy of Education

Previously, it was mentioned that experimentalist believe we can know experiences only from the physical and social world. Idealists state that we receive ideas only, not experiences; nor can we know what the real world is like in whole or in part as realists indicate. Idealism is an idea centred philosophy of education. Mind is real and needs to receive nourishment through quality ideas in different academic disciplines. There are numerous tutorial programmes with computer use that stress learners achieving important concepts and generalizations. Knowledge objectives predominate, according to idealism as a philosophy of teaching and learning. Ediger (1986) wrote the following:

Idealism is a more traditional approach in making decisions as compared to experimentalism and existentialism. According to idealists, individualists cannot know the world as it truly is in terms of an objective reality. Each person, however, obtains ideas pertaining to objects and items in the environment. The mind brings order to what is observed and seen. Thus, of all facets of human development that is significant to develop, the mind or intellectual achievement must come first. Rich learning experiences will need to be in evidence to guide pupils to achieve maximum development mentally. Thus experiences may well be selected in terms of leading pupils to attain universal ideas and knowledge of the Absolute (God). These universal ideas need seeking and finding. Any person may not achieve perfect understanding of these universal ideas and of God. However, each person may continually move closer in achieving ideals of universal ideas and of the absolute.

From the thinking of idealists, the following implications apply for teaching and learning:

1. broad generalizations need emphasizing that have much use to the learner in terms of mental and moral development;
2. quality ideals for pupils to emulate need adequate emphasis in the school curriculum;
3. intellectual objectives should receive primary stress in the curriculum;
4. quality course work in literature and history, in particular, should guide pupils to achieve worthy generalizations;
5. abstract ideas are more important to emphasize as compared to the concrete and the semiconcrete.

Key ideas in understanding idealism in teaching and learning are written by Bigge (1982) in the following statements:

The heart of idealism is the belief that basic reality consists of ideas, thoughts, minds or substantive selves, not physical matter. Since priority is given to minds, minds have bodies, but bodies do not have minds. Idealism usually carries with its view the ideas of the subsistence (the super-existence) of God, who also is basically mind or self. The universe is an expression of intelligence and will; its order is due to an external, spiritual reality. For idealists, people are just good-active substantive minds; they are absolutely real selves endowed with free will or genuine moral choice. This philosophy has ancient roots; it dates back to Socrates (469-399 BC) and Plato (427-347).

Idealism is really idea-ism. The source of this title is based on Platonic thought. For Plato, ideas alone were genuinely real; they consisted of immaterial essences. That which people perceive is a shadow of reality; each thing that they perceive gets its existence from its Thingness; an idea. A book is a book because of its being more or less an imperfect replica of Bookness. A woman is a woman because she is a replica of

Womaness. Plato's assumed worlds of "eternal verities" consisted of the True, the Good, and the Beautiful.

We can trace the development of idealism by listing some of the leading philosophers who contributed to this position and stated a leading idea that each has contributed to the philosophy. Socrates believed that children are born with knowledge already in their minds, but they need help to recall this innate knowledge. Plate contributed the idea of ideas, which are the universal forms of all existing things and are the essence of reality. St. Augustine (350-430) held a dualistic (mind-body) theory of humanity within which the mind or soul is the set of the force of goodness.

What then are the implications of idealism for teaching and learning in the classroom involving computer use? We have seen selected excellent software packages which stress an idea centred curriculum. It seems as if for each academic area, there are tutorials which might well assist any pupil to achieve subject matter knowledge.

These software packages should assist pupils to

1. achieve abstract content which is challenging and yet attainable;
2. learn content in depth with emphasis placed upon mental development of pupils;
3. acquire subject matter which makes sense and has meaning;
4. relate relevant content from an academic centred curriculum;
5. attain vital facts, concepts, and generalizations in each academic discipline.

An idea centred curriculum might also guide pupils to use what has been learned in problem solving. This belief assists in relating idealism with experimentalism.

Existentialism and the Curriculum

Existentialism are very much concerned about the every day life and its anxieties of individuals. Individuals are concerned with choices that need to be made regardless if the desire is there to make these decisions. There is dread, fear, anxiety, and uncertainty in making choices. Many existentialists believe life to be absurd and ridiculous. There is dread in choosing when so many alternatives are available in the making of these choices. People do not live in a subject centred world, nor in a world of science. Rather they live in an open ended world where there are no standards in and of themselves. These standards, rules and regulations, need to be developed. Human beings make their own world; there are no absolutes nor are there given rules to live by. People, past and present, have developed standards to go by in life, but these are human made in an open environment where people, individually and collectively, develop the kind of society they wish to have. Pertaining to existentialism, Ozman and Craver (1990) wrote:

> Because the individual human is so important as the creator of ideas, existentialists maintain that education should focus upon individual human reality. It should deal with the individual as a unique being in the world, not only as a creator of ideas, but as a living, feeling being. Most philosophies... existentialists charge, tend to focus upon only as a cognitive being. The individual is this, but he is also a feeling, aware person, and existentialists think that this side deserves attention.

Which implications in the curriculum might follow some of the tenets of existentialism?

1. pupils individually need to choose freely, from among alternatives, those learning activities which are purposeful and meaningful;
2. content in the curriculum should reflect human feelings of loneliness, alienation, anxiety, and tension.
3. personal feelings of the pupil should be reflected in ongoing lessons and units of study. These feelings might well be expressed in art and construction projects, as well as of personal writings of learners.

The pupil needs to realize that choices do need to be made. If others make decisions for the personal self, choices are still being made, but the individual has abdicated responsibility in the decision making arena. Choices made do involve dilemma decisions, but authentic decisions must be made. Coercion is definitely not a part of the decision making philosophy of existentialists. Quality decisions made do not always make for good human relations. Alienation may also be an end result. The individual always needs to consider the consequences of choices made. Moral decisions made in a free environment is the goal of existentialists. Individuals should remember they are responsible for choices made; no one else can assume this responsibility. Choice are subjective, not objective by any means.

With technology in the curriculum, existentialism advocates

1. individuals selecting from among others computer programmes to complete. The individual should also choose which tasks to engage in when additional forms of technology are used;
2. the human condition with all of its uncertainties and anxieties should be stressed in the technology curriculum;
3. the pupil needs to have ample opportunities to study situations in which dilemmas are present. Decision making is not clear cut nor an absolute. Content in technology can emphasize these ideas;
4. the learner needs to express his/her feelings in diverse projects and activities. Thus a variety of writing experiences, fine arts and practical arts activities, speaking and reading learning opportunities, as well as listening may be stressed as evaluation techniques as well as enrichment activities in the technology curriculum;

5. heavy pupil involvement and choice in the technology curriculum should always be in evidence with existentialism as a driving philosophy in education.

Realism and the Technology Curriculum

Realists are strong advocates of individuals knowing in whole or in part what the real world is like. Their model comes from the world of science and mathematics. Precision and extreme accuracy are major tenets of realism as a philosophy of education. Thus the realist is strongly interested in having pupils achieve precise, measurably stated objectives in each curriculum area. With these kinds of objectives, carefully chosen by teachers and other educators, pupils do or do not attain each objective as a result of instruction. Learning activities selected by the teacher harmonizes with what pupils are to learn as contained in the stated objective(s). Evaluation techniques need to be aligned with the stated objectives. Validity is then in evidence in testing and measurement. Reliability needs to stress test-retest, split half, and/or alternative forms of appraisal. Results from pupils tests should indicate numerical data such as percentile ranks, per cent of items correct, standard deviations, quartile deviations, and standardized scores. Subjectivity in testing is definitely not wanted. Rather objectivity in testing is advocated to determine what any one pupil has learned as a result of teaching.

Pertaining to realism, Wild (1955) wrote the following:

The child, of course, should be interested in what he is learning. But it does not follow that whatever the child is interested in is, therefore, valuable. This is absurd. The skill of the elementary teacher lies in eliciting the interest of the child in the right things, especially in grasping the truth for its own sake. At the early stages no psychological or rhetorical technique should be neglected which is capable of strengthening this urge. When a mathematical principle has been understood, the child's attention should be drawn at once to the problem this enables him to solve. No opportunity should be lost to point out the principles of pure science which underlie modern technology. Language and grammar should be taught at essential phases of that mysterious process of apprehension by which the actual structure of things is mentally reflected and expressed, and by which such knowledge is achieved.

Realists do place very strong emphasis upon the following in teaching and learning situations:

1. carefully selected ends for pupils to achieve need to be written in precise, measurable terms;
2. learning opportunities chosen by the teacher align with the ends or objectives mentioned in number 1 above;
3. pupil achievement in having attained the precise objectives are measurable and presented in numerical terms;
4. the models of mathematics and science with its accuracy and specificity should be incorporated into the curriculum;
5. research studies can provide much data on what learners should study such as, for example, which words pupils should master in spelling. Many excellent studies have been made which indicate the words pupils use must frequently in functional writing. Words that are misspelled in these writings provide a scientific basis for determining practical words to be chosen by the teacher for pupil mastery.

Technology needs to be matched with the chosen objectives of instruction in lesson plans and units of study. After the use of technology in teaching and learning situations, the teacher may measure what pupils have learned. The results are given in numerical terms, not vague subjective data. The objective results may be reported to parents to indicate learner achievement in the school curriculum.

Leadership in Technology Use

Teachers need to be and are leaders in curriculum development. They select objectives, learning activities, and appraisal procedures. Teachers organise the classroom for instruction. Organisational work includes grouping pupils for instruction, disciplining pupils, as well as devising a schedule for teaching. Technology is definitely involved in making curricular decisions. For example, there should be an ample number of software programmes in the learning activities section to guide pupils to achieve objectives. Definite leadership skills are necessary here. In addition to the classroom teacher, the principal plays a vital role in curriculum development.

Ritchie (1996) wrote the following pertaining to reasons why the use of technology is minimal in schools:

- A lack of administrative support
- Inadequate staff development and technological support
- Low quantity, quality, and access of technologies in the classroom
- Nonexistent or cursory plans for adopting and implementing technology into a school
- The failure to allocate a technology coordinator to help train teachers and coordinate the technologies
- A lack of funds and personnel to maintain equipment
- Continual assessment of content acquisition through traditional methods
- Establishment of a broad participatory clientele to establish a technology culture (Hoffman, 1996)

From the above statements, it is quite clear that school administrators need to understand and value technological use in the classroom. School administrators should perceive the necessity of implementing technology use in the classroom so that pupils may achieve more optimally. No doubt, there are school administrators who lack quality experiences with technology and therefore do not see the need for pupils experiencing learning activities involving technology. Each principal and supervisor should avail themselves in learning more about technology and how to integrate its use into the school curriculum. Talking to and learning from classroom teachers should assist the school administrator in realizing the importance of technology in a modern elementary curriculum. Staff development programmes in using technology in the curriculum should be in the offing. Teachers and administrators need to realize the importance of an updated curriculum. The school of today and the work place of tomorrow should not be in isolation from each other, but rather become integrated entities. Definite goals in inservice education using technology are musts! These goals and experiences for participants need to be chosen carefully. Relevance and importance are two concepts that need careful consideration when inservice education programmes are developed and implemented. The goals of the workshop need to be clearly stated and should be cooperatively developed by workshop participants. There should be a large group session to hear a speaker or two who introduce vital inservice education goals. In the large group session, participants need to identify problem areas pertaining to the use of technology. Cooperative endeavours and committee work should follow to solve identified problems from the large group session. Consultants need to be available to assist in clarifying ideas and raising important questions to consider. A hands on approach should be in the offing. Individual endeavours need to also be pursued in the inservice education programme. Participants individually have concerns that need addressing with consultant assistance. There should be opportunities to try out what has been studied in the inservice education programme to the level of application in the regular public school classroom. Feedback from the classroom to participants in the inservice education programme is a must!

There need to be definite plans to integrate technology into the school curriculum. This should not be left to chance, but rather quality goals and plans have been developed to use technology to its fullest in teaching and learning situations. Teachers need to have easy access to technology in lesson plan and teaching unit construction. A trained and educated coordinator of technology use can assist teachers to educate children for more optimal achievement. The coordinator of technology needs to develop good human relations with teachers with the latter having access readily to technology.

Adequate money needs to be budgeted and used to develop a curriculum with technology as a guiding principal. The lay public needs to be informed continuously about the merits of using technology in the classroom to assist each pupil to achieve optimally use with pupils, teachers, and administrators indicating its importance to child growth and development in the school setting.

Maskin (1996) wrote the following:

Promoters of computers in the classroom claim that exposing pupils to Web sites, e-mail, and newsgroups promises more than the means of securing a job in the next century. Technology boosters also predict that the use and mastery of the internet and the World Wide Web will produce affective changes that can be measured to produce increased student self-esteem and confidence. Whether working at home or in school, as an individual or in a cooperative learning or team setting, students will become 'infotectives', *i.e.* independent thinkers, researchers, inventors, inquirers, capable of solving problems that often required the active direction of a teacher of supervisor...

In expanding the learning environment to include data bases, computer networks, and other library resources throughout the world, the internet makes it possible for students to shape their own education. Once the easy accessing protocols are learned, the student can dive into these resources in the comfort of his or her home and/or library without the constant supervision and intervention of the teacher. Lao Tzui's' dictum. "He who teaches least teaches best," describes a student centred teaching, learning, and assessment environment in which the student can access information from multiple perspectives and learn to use this information to solve complex problems.

Freedom, however, also opens up the possibility of choice. The emerging information technologies can just as easily be used to access sports trivia as they can explore issues being debated in Congress or at the World Bank. Many students, if left to their devices, might choose to spend hours surfing the 'Net for their own enjoyment rather than using it to complete a school assignment. The job of the teacher, therefore, is to involve students, individually or in teams, in internet projects that are fun to do and skill enhancing. Students exposed early on to such educational endeavours are more likely to feel comfortable and confident in Drucker's knowledge based society...

I am convinced that Internet connectivity empowers students, gives them research advantage, and generally gets them excited about learning.

We are truly in an information age in which there are so many outstanding sources of content for pupil acquisition. Pupils need to have ample opportunities to secure a variety of subject matter on a topic. It does cost money to have the latest of technology in our schools. But can we afford to be without it? Pupils today, in a few years, will be in the work place where the information age will even more be clearly defined as compared to today. Pupils of every race, creed, and religion must have the chances in an equitable manner to be able to use the latest in data securing sources. The upper income level pupils will have these opportunities of obtaining information through World Wide Web and Internet in the home setting. Other pupils also should have equality of opportunity to use state of the art sources to obtain information.

Pertaining to the future of technology, Mehlinger (1996) wrote the following:

Without going into detail regarding specific pieces of hardware. I can say with confidence that schools should expect more *integration, interaction and intelligence* from future technology. In their early days in school, computers and video were regarded as separate entities, and it was assumed they would stay that way. In fact, we can expect a continuing integration of these technologies. Voice, data, and images will be brought together into one package. One current example of this process is desktop video. In a single, relatively inexpensive unit, one has telephone (voice), computer (data storage and manipulation), and video (sending and receiving moving images) capabilities. Those who use the machine can talk to people at a distance, exchange documents, work collaboratively, and even see collaborators on the screen.

Technology will also become more interactive. In the field of distance learning, rather than strictly rely on one-way video and two way communication, teachers and students will see another simultaneously, thereby making distance learning more like face-to-face classroom interaction. Computer based instruction will also be designed to respond to learners' interests and abilities, giving them greater control over what they need to learn and the pace at which they will learn it. And computer searches, which can be bewildering to the casual observer, will become easier and more responsive to what a user needs. Greater interactivity will make instructional programmes even more powerful than they are today.

Finally, technology will have greater intelligence. This intelligence will be displayed in several ways. First, the technology will have more features and greater capacity. Second, it will have the capability to learn from the user, so that it can customize its services to fit the user's learning style and interest. Future technology will provide not only data bases but knowledge bases. And technology will be able to stay abreast of that information most valued to the user and alert him or her to its availability.

Integration, interaction, and intelligence. These are three features we can expect of technology in the future. And they will change the way technology is employed in schools.

In Summary

From the psychology of learning, there are numerous criteria recommended for teaching pupils. These are that interest needs to be developed within pupils for learning, purpose should be there on the learner's part to achieve, meaning should be inherent in ongoing lessons and units of study, relationship of knowledge is salient in the instructional arena, individual differences among pupils need to be provided for, and good attitudes need adequate emphasis.

Four philosophies of education were discussed and need to be appraised so that the best one(s) are used to meet individual pupil learning styles. These philosophies are experimentalism with its stress upon pupil problem solving; idealism with its emphasis upon an idea centred curriculum advocating learner's achieving abstract subject matter; existentialism with values placed upon the individual pupil selecting, from among alternatives, learning opportunities to pursue; and realism with its stress upon pupils achieving measurable stated objectives.

The future seemingly looks bright for use of technology in the classroom. The use of World Wide Web and Internet, e-mail, faxing and electronic bulletin board, among others, will guide pupils to attain vital objectives of instruction. Desktop videos, as a truly modern device in technology, integrate voice, sound, and the pictorial.

REFERENCES

Bigge, Morris L. (1982). *Educational Philosophies for Teachers.* Columbus, Ohio: Charles E. Merrill Publishing Company, pp. 25 and 26.

Choice or Chance (1984). Chicago, Illinois: Rand Mc Nally and Company.

Ediger, Marlow (1995). *Philosophy in Curriculum Development.* Kirksville, Missouri: Simpson Publishing Company, pp. 86-87.

Ediger, Marlow (1986). *Social Studies Curriculum in Elementary School.* Third Edition. Kirksville. Missouri, p. 241.

Ediger, Marlow and Digumarti Bhaskara Rao (2000). *Teaching Social Studies Successfully.* New Delhi, India: Discovery Publishing House.

Eichelberger, Tony R. (1889). *Disciplined Inquiry: Understanding and Doing Educational Research.* White Plains, New York: Longman, Inc., p. 11.

Hoffman, Bob (1996). "School Technology Integration: An Automated Needs Assessment and Planning Tool." in *Technology and Teacher Education Annual*, edited by Robin, Price, Willis, and Willis. Charlottesville, Virginia: Association for the Advancement of Computing in Education.

Maskin, Melvin (1996). "Infotectives on the Infobahn: Designing Internet-Aided Projects for the Social Studies Classroom, *National Association of Secondary School Principal's Bulletin*, Vol. 80, No. 582, pp. 59-69.

Mehlinger, Howard D. (1996). "School Reform in the Information Age," *Phi Delta Kappan*, Vol. 77, No. 6, pp. 405-406.

Morris, Van Cleve and Young Pai (1976). *Philosophy and the American School*: Houghton Mifflin Company, p. 378.

Ozman, Howard, and Samuel Craver (1990). *Philosophical Foundations and Education*. Fourth Edition. Columbus, Ohio: Merrill Publishing Company, p. 249.

Ritchie, Donn (1996), "The Administrative Role in Integration of Technology," *Bulletin of the National Association of Secondary School Principals*, Vol. 80, No. 582, p. 43.

Rose, Stephen A., and Phyllis Maxey Fernlund (1997), "Using Technology for Powerful Social Studies Learning. *Social Education*. Vol. 61, No. 3, pp. 161-162.

Wild, John (1955). *Modern Philosophies of Education*. Chicago, Illinois: The National Society for the Study of Education, p. 31.

7

Writing in the Science Curriculum

Pupils need to become quality communicators of content in writing. Why? Scientists in a laboratory setting must be able to write their findings in an accurate, objective approach so that effective communication among experts, as well as others, is in evidence. Not being able to communicate effectively in writing would greatly hinders scientific achievement in sequence on a continuing basis. Thus, in poorly developed written communication, scientists could not benefit from each other's research and findings. It behooves the teacher to encourage, assist, and motivate each pupil to do as well as possible in writing in ongoing science units of study.

Pupils may engage in writing on an individual or committee basis. Pertaining to committee or cooperative learning endeavours, Ediger (1997) wrote:

Cooperative learning is receiving considerable emphasis in curriculum development. It is difficult to say how cooperative learning is different from the earlier term "committee endeavours" stressed in curriculum development. Presently, it appears that most writers and speakers in education recommend using cooperative learning rather heavily in the classroom. Thus, pupils in a class work cooperatively in projects, activities, and experiences. The teacher becomes a guide or assistant to help learners achieve as much as possible. It is important here to emphasize that pupils work as a unit, not separately. Quality group dynamics becomes salient in cooperative learning. Learners then need to achieve goals and be goal centred. Competition among individuals is deemphasized and cooperation is salient. Individuals may work on different tasks in a term setting; however, these endeavours should represent cooperation in goal attainment.

Why is cooperative learning important? Presently, as well as in the future work place, individuals will be asked to work harmoniously with others. The individual who cannot work well with others will be handicapped. There are people from diverse cultures and abilities in any work place. Thus a pupil presently should be able to work with children of different values and talents. Being able to accept others is of utmost importance. Pupils individually need to be responsible to contribute optimally in cooperative endeavours. They need to think of themselves as a part of a group, not as competitive individuals. At issue here is how much time should be placed upon cooperative learning as compared to individual achievement. To think about individual endeavours in the curriculum, one must admit this is also important. Each person interacts with others and yet also needs to be able to use spare time wisely on an individual basis. A person is not a member of a group always but is also a person who has unique interests, needs, and purposes.

Writing and the Pupil

The science teacher needs to determine where each pupil is presently in achievement in writing. At this starting point, the teacher must guide learners on an individual basis to attain optimally and in a sequential manner.

A. Writing Experience Charts in Science

Early primary grade pupils tend to enjoy writing experience charts. A cooperative teacher who supervised a student teacher of mine taught a unit on *Animals in Our Lives*. She had three goldfish in an aquarium, tadpoles in a jar, a frog in a terrarium, a small greater snake in a different terrarium and a pet canary in a bird cage. Pupils observed the goldfish carefully as they swam in the aquarium. Pupils were then asked to present ideas on what they saw to the teacher who in return recorded in writing observations presented. The following sentences, among others, were given in which first grade learners could see talk written down and experience writing:

1. The gold fish swam rapidly.
2. The bright colours mixed with the sunlight.
3. Water in the aquarium has bubbles inside of it.
4. Fish come up to breathe air.
5. It is fun to watch the fish being fed.

The numerals were then removed from the above experience chart and pupils read the content with teacher guidance. The teacher pointed to the words as the young learners orally read the content together with the teacher. There were numerous pupils who could not read the subject matter initially, but developed confidence to do so as the teacher patiently pronounced the words sequentially in the group exercise using the experience chart. The experience chart was saved and posted on the wall. Pupils could then view the chart as the need arose. A week later, the teacher again read the contents of the chart with the children involved. Several asked to read it individually to the entire class. This developed considerable enthusiasm. The teacher announced to the class that anyone wishing to read the contents of the chart to her (the teacher) should do so at any time. At this point and stage of achievement, most of these first grade pupils read the subject matter on the chart, making very few errors. This chart and later ones developed were saved for learners to reread at their own convenience.

With the use of the experience chart approach in teaching writing, pupils can see talk written down. Thus what is said orally can be printed with the use of abstract symbols in grapheme-phoneme relationships. The experience chart concept of teaching reading is based upon learners having a personal experience. In this situation, the experience was to look at goldfish. Later experience charts would be based upon pupils seeing tadpoles, frogs, a snake, and a canary. This brought to the attention of pupils, fish, amphibians, reptiles, and birds as sequential classification of animals with backbones. Still later, the teacher brought her pet cat to class to show a mammal.

With concrete experiences of viewing lifelike, real animals, pupils began to use language to describe what was viewed. The use of oral communication was then inherent. Pupils listened to the ideas presented by others. The content that resulted was printed in neat, manuscript letters by the teacher. Learners then read the content orally with teacher guidance as the latter pointed to the words and phrases within each sentence. Thus oral communication, listening, writing, and reading were experienced by each learner. The four language arts areas then become an inherent part of the science unit currently being studied.

When pupils are ready, they should write their own experience charts. This activity can be appropriate on any grade level.

Art work may well be related to writing experiences for pupils. Ediger and Rao (1996, pages 91-92) wrote:

Learning activities involving art work can do much to enrich the elementary school science curriculum. Thus, the science teacher must provide a variety of learning experiences involving art in the science programme.

1. Developing murals. Pupils in a committee may plan and develop a mural pertaining to an ongoing unit of study in science. Thus, if pupils, for example, are studying a unit on "Animals with Backbones," they may decide upon scenes involving—
   (a) diverse kinds of fish;
   (b) amphibians, *e.g.* toads and frogs;

(c) reptiles, *e.g.* snakes and turtles;

(d) various kinds of birds;

(e) mammals, *e.g.* human beings, monkeys chimpanzees, gorillas.

2. Developing friezes. A series of pictures developed by a committee of pupils is inherent in cooperative planning and implementing the frieze concept in art work. A variety of media should be avȁilable to pupils when working on a frieze. Thus, caryons, coloured chalk, water colours, colored pencils and finger paints should be readily accessible at the frieze centre. If pupils, for example, are studying a unit on "Animals Without Backbones", they may develop a series of illustrations (a frieze) on—

(a) protozoans, *e.g.* the amoeba, the paramecium, and the euglena.

(b) porifera (sponges);

(c) coelenteratas, *e.g.* hydras, jellyfish, coral, and sea anemones;

(d) platyhelminthes (flatworms) *e.g.* planarian, flukes, and tapeworms;

(e) aschelminthes (roundworms), *e.g.* hookworms, ascaris, and trichinella;

(f) annelida (segmented worms) *e.g.* earthworm and sandworm;

(g) echinodermata (spiny animals) *e.g.* star fish, the sea urchin, the sea cucumber, and the sand dollar;

(h) molusca (shellfish) *e.g.* clams, scallops, oysters, snails, and slugs;

(i) arthropods, e.g. shrimp, lobsters, crayfish, and crabs. Insects are also members of this phylum—praying mantis, grasshopper, walking stick, dragonflies, ladybugs, and potato beetles.

B. Outlining Content in Science

Outlining content read from the basal or other reference source might well assist pupils to be able to organise information better in terms of sequence. A quality outline should possess the following parts:

1. The title
2. Roman numerals to show the main ideas or divisions
3. Capital letters under each main idea to show the relationship of these subdivisions with the main idea
4. Details with ordered numerals under each subdivision to show relationships between the subdivision and the related details.

In outlining content, such as from the basal textbook in science, pupils may perceive the relationship of subordinate ideas to the main idea, the details to the subordinate idea, and the general sequence of subject matter. A pupil that focuses too much upon isolated facts tends to forget content sooner as compared to those who perceive that broader ideas exist such as subordinate and main ideas. Then too, broader ideas tend to become a part of the general repertoire of the learner sooner as compared to the acquisition of isolated facts. Thus, there is a structure of knowledge is science for the learner when he/she perceives that key ideas can be selected and subordinate content and details can be related rather readily to the main ideas. We recommend that when pupils are ready, not before, they experience practice in outlining subject matter, not for the sake of doing so, but to perceive knowledge as being related.

A quality outline on a purposeful topic provides the learner with an excellent tool to present an oral report to others in the classroom setting. The pupil should never read ideas from an outline, but use the ideas therein to present well organised subject matter to listeners. Thus, if the learner forgets sequential content in the report, he/she may then refer to the outline. Quality organisation of content assists the listener to acquire what is being presented. If an oral report contains randomly presented ideas, the chances are that comprehension by listeners will be difficult.

Pupils may receive practice in reading content in science that is poorly organised and rearrange the sentences so that coherence is in evidence. Noticing the differences between the two is important.

Writing Results From Science Experiments

A very useful writing experience for pupils is to write up science experiments that have been or will be performed in ongoing units of study. We believe that a plan developed by the teacher with pupil involvement will aid in writing that which is clear and distinct. First of all, the experiment needs to have a title which is meaningful to readers. If pupils are studying a unit or partial unit on water erosion of soil, a science experiment that is salient might well be entitled "Water and Soil Erosion". A problem then needs to be stated. The problem should be written clearly so that related information may be located as solutions. Hazy problem areas do not lend themselves to finding needed answers. A clearly worded problem might be the following: How does rainfall affect the soil in our school yard? Learners might then brainstorm answers to this question. No value judgement should be made of contributions of individual pupils. Respect for the thinking of others is necessary to generate ideas. The answers proposed in brainstorming should be recorded on the chalkboard to avoid unnecessary duplications. Higher levels of cognition are involved when pupils continue to offer answers. Initially, it probably is relatively easy to offer answers to the identified problem or question. After brainstorming, pupils need to ascertain which answers are acceptable and which are not. Science experiments should be performed in the classroom to determine the affects of water upon soil as well as observing in the out-of-doors what happens to soil with different levels of intensity of falling rain. As many variables as possible must be observed too, such as the slope of the land, the covering (grass) of the soil, and the kind of soil (clay, sandy, loam, among others). Inside the classroom, two boxes of equivalent soil with equal slope may be used initially. A similar amount of water should be poured over each box containing the soil. The only variable tested here is that one box has a grass covering over the soil whereas the other box does not. The amount of runoff of the soil for each box may be determined with a small container as broad as each box at the base to catch the eroded soil. Other variables to test for include different cover crops, different kinds of soil, as well as different amounts of water with variable intensity poured over each box.

These activities can also be used in testing the different answers given in brainstorming:

1. reading from diverse sources which shed light on water erosion of soil;
2. viewing audiovisual aids on causes and prevention of erosion of soil;
3. listening to qualified resource persons;
4. doing additional experiments and observing demonstrations;
5. making models of soil preservation including terracing, strip cropping, and trees/vegetative coverings to prevent erosion in its diverse forms.

Answers to questions should be viewed as tentative with chances of making necessary modifications as the need arises. Each step discussed above should be written with clarity and precision. Thus the problem or question, the brainstormed ideas, the data gathering, and needed modifications sections should be written with meaning and comprehension. Quality writing assists in communicating ideas more effectively.

A long standing debate has been in evidence in the teaching of science as to should it stress processes or products. A very popular approach in teaching science is Science—*A Process Approach* (SAPA) developed by the American Association for the Advancement of Science (no data given); their advocated objectives are the following processes:

1. observing;
2. recognizing and using number relations;
3. measuring;
4. recognizing and using space time relations;
5. classifying;
6. communicating;
7. inferring;
8. predicting;
9. defining operationally;
10. formulating hypotheses
11. interpreting data
12. controlling variables;
13. experimenting.

The science teacher may stress the above named SAPA with or without using their materials of instruction. For example, objective number one above which is observing is very important in all science units of study. Here, the teacher may emphasize pupils observing a science experiment and all the sequential steps therein. The teacher may then appraise if pupils are observing carefully. This may be determined by teachers viewing attentiveness of learners during an experiment. Pupils might reveal their observational skills by writing up what happened sequentially in the ongoing experiment.

D. Writing Book Reports

Summarizing what has been read from a library book directly related to an ongoing science unit can be highly educational for pupils. The learner should have had the opportunity to choose his/her own book to read, from among others, at a reading centre. There are several kinds of writing activities that can be implemented here. The pupil needs to select which procedure to use when writing about subject matter read from a library book. Thus, the pupils may choose from among the following:

1. writing a certain number of main ideas covered in the chosen book;
2. writing what was perceived to be the most interesting content contained in the reading material;
3. writing one or more paragraphs pertaining to the central idea contained in the library book;
4. writing questions that remain unanswered pertaining to the content;
5. writing a different beginning or ending if the contents of the library book are highly creative, such as the book *Miss Pickerel on Mars*.

Writing summaries pertaining to content read from library books should encourage, not destroy interest, in reading and writing content in science. The teacher should evaluate achievement here and in all writing experiences based on the following criteria:

1. use standards that assist the learner to notice that which needs to be improved upon;
2. have reasonable standards for each pupil, not excessively difficult nor at too low a level of achievement;
3. do not emphasize too many correlations for any one pupil to make, lest the involved child is overwhelmed with corrections that need to be made;
4. focus upon ideas in the written product; not exclusively upon the mechanics of writing such as spelling, punctuation, and grammar;
5. emphasize clarity of ideas expressed, not quantity in content written.

It is important for teachers to have conferences with pupils, one on one, to assist learners to improve over previous attempts at written work. The conference should stress caring for the pupil in becoming a better writer. Negative criticism must be avoided in the conference setting. A positive attitude toward the learner and his/her ability to improve in writing in all school endeavours is a must. Ediger (1996) wrote:

Relevant principles of psychology in teaching and learning must be followed when pupils engage in ongoing units of study... in the science curriculum. Thus, experiences for pupils should follow these standards or criteria:

1. learning activities should be interesting and meaningful;
2. pupils must have needed background information and possess adequate readiness for new units of study;
3. learners should perceive purpose in learning in ongoing units of study;
4. each pupil should be guided to achieve optimal development in understandings, skills, an attitudinal objectives;
5. learner progress must be continuously evaluated to determine progress in achieving stated objectives.

E. Journal Writing in Science

Pupils need to be given time to engage in journal writing, this provides opportunities for learners to reflect upon what has been learned in ongoing science units and lessons. Journal entries may be dated. What is written in the journal is up to the pupil. A pupil may then write what transpired in a science experiment or demonstration. The learner may wish to focus upon salient ideas discussed in a committee setting. With reflection, the involved learner will remember better what has been learned due to thinking upon key ideas or concepts stressed in science. The pupil might desire to write about attitudes and interests developed in science as a result of teaching and learning experiences.

Should the teacher appraise the quality of these journal entries? If not, how does a teacher know if the time devoted to journal writing is worthwhile and assists the learner to attain relevant objectives? If the teacher appraises the quality of journal writing, should the contents be graded? These and other vital questions need careful consideration.

We would suggest that teachers encourage pupils to share their writings. This can be done by sharing content written with the teacher on a voluntary basis. Pupils might also meet in committees to share what has been written. It is best if pupils are not coerced to show what was written in the journal. However, pupil may waste time and pretend he/she is writing, but is day dreaming or writing irrelevant content. We believe the teacher can and must observe pupils to notice that achievement is taking place in all learning opportunities. A general overview in observing learner achievement may suffice in appraising pupil progress in writing journal entries. The teacher needs to be a good observer and use quality criteria to appraise pupil progress. A listing of criteria may assist the teacher to make justifiable decisions pertaining to pupil journal writing. Among others, these include the following:

1. time on task is vital;
2. conscientious and judicious statements are a must;
3. proper order of written subject matter is salient;
4. clarity of content is necessary;
5. accurate mechanics in writing are needed to the degree it makes the written content more meaningful.

There should be a variety of kinds of learning opportunities in writing so that pupils feel that written work is utilitarian and purposeful.

F. Writing Diary Entries

Pupils individually or in committees need to have ample opportunities to write on a day-to-day basis what was learned in a science lesson. Each entry should be dated. By writing what was learned on a daily basis in science, writers review previously acquired information. With review, subject matter learned will be retained for a longer period of time than would otherwise be the case. Pupils should participate on a rotating basis in writing these diary entries. The following are examples of diary entries written by a committee of learners:

October One. The teacher explained to use the differences between sheet and gulley erosion. Emphasis was also placed upon the amount of top soil lost each year due to erosion. Farm crop yields decrease when rich top soil is not available for the growing of wheat, soyabeans, and corn, among other grains. Marginal and tilled hilly land, in particular, are subject to increased erosion.

October two. We went outdoors to notice gulley erosion beginnings on our playground. We levelled the soil and seeded grass to avoid erosion. We then came into the classroom to watch a video-tape on "Preventing Soil Erosion." Before observing the video, we hypothesized on ways to prevent soil erosion. During the video, we were asked to list and describe different ways to prevent or minimize soil erosion as presented in the video. These ways include using terraces, seeding grass and planning trees, as well as emphasizing strip cropping, among others.

The teacher may discuss with the entire class what might be added to each diary entry. These entries should be kept so that pupils might use these for review. Individual or committee members' names may appear on each page of diary entries and bound for future reference. Hopefully, the learning opportunity will increase learner interest, purpose, and meaning for writing in science.

G. Writing Log Entries

Pupils may review and combine the diary entries so that a log may be written. A log covers a longer period of time in terms of lesson content as compared to diary entries. Thus a log may pertain to recording what was learned within a week. The diary entries then become a part of the log. Individuals and committees who record the log entries must read carefully each diary entry so that broader generalizations may be written such as in a log. Log entries should be bound together with the diary entries so that pupils might review and rehearse what had been learned previously. Log entries provide a good basis in reviewing for an oncoming test.

Standards to follow in writing log entries include the following:

1. ideas should be specific enough so that misinterpretation is not possible;
2. quality human relations need to be stressed in any committee endeavours;
3. appropriate order of content is necessary so that sequence is in evidence;
4. correct spelling of words, punctuation, indentation of paragraphs, and grammar should be in evidence in order to communicate effectively. However, the focal point is on ideas in the logs, not the mechanics of writing;
5. log writing must encourage an increased desire to write rather than writing being perceived as a chore.

If pupils are to become good writers, writing should be emphasized across the curriculum. The curriculum area of science provides its many opportunities for pupils to become good writers. The are numerous purposes in writing in science. The author here recommends that pupils participate actively and fully in written work in ongoing lessons and units of study in science.

Use Word Processors

One of the greatest boon to writing has been the use of the word processor. The word processor indeed eliminates much drudgery attached to writing. The mistakes made in typing can quickly be corrected on the monitor before a final copy is sent through the printer. One can secure the desired copy, reading it on the monitor, before printing occurs. A perfect copy may then result even if a person's typing is not the best. A spell check programme eliminates spelling errors in a hurry without retyping any part of the document. There are limitations here in that the computer does not catch errors in homonyms nor in selected other kinds of errors such as in punctuation or capitalization. The user of the word processor still needs to be able to proof read typed content carefully and oh so carefully. However, spelling errors can all be taken care of in a very short time indeed with a spell check programme. Typing errors can be taken care of quickly be looking to see what is on the monitor and making needed revisions when proofing. We find it enjoyable to use a word processor in typing manuscript content each day. One can make much headway in typing with a personal computer that is very user friendly. A person who can type using the old typewriter can learn very quickly to use a word processor and be amazed at its capabilities!

Pupils who use word processors, when ready, feel ownership of the tasks involved thereon. The pupil with teacher assistance determines the content to be put into the computer. He/she sequences the content to be typed. Revisions are made in terms of the writer's goals. When changes need to be made such as rearrangement of ideas in the typing, this can be done quickly. No longer does a writer need to start all over in typing a page if a single error has been made. White out does not need to be used in making corrections as was true of typewriter use. The writing curriculum must be updated so that each learner can benefit from modern technology and its applications. Will word processors, the following conclusions may well be emphasized:

1. writing tends to be more enjoyable since errors made can quickly and conveniently be corrected with user friendly technology;
2. the rearrangement of ideas for quality sequence can be rapidly implemented, making it unnecessary to start over again in the typing process;
3. pupils may feel that what is done using the word processor is completely in their hands. The pupil gives the commands to the computer and completely controls what will follow in terms of content and the mechanics of writing;
4. content typed can involve diverse purposes such as formal and creative writing. Each of the purposes

discussed throughout this manuscript pertaining to writing may be emphasized using the word processor;

5. pupils individually or in dyads may write using the word processor depending upon goals stressed in writing in science. Goals may stress individual as well as group or committee endeavours in the curriculum.

In Closing

The science teacher needs to provide a variety of writing activities for pupils. This is necessary to provide for individual differences. Pupils should be guided to become increasingly proficient in writing. One cannot expect a pupil to blossom immediately into becoming a good writer. Rather, sequentially, each pupil can build a repertoire of writing skills. By comparing a pupil's past written product with his present written work, the teacher can notice the degree to which a learner is achieving more fully. Writing is a basic in the curriculum. The science teacher should incorporate writing experiences when it assists pupils to acquire more subject matter content. Acquisition of facts, concepts, generalizations, principles, and laws of science are vital. So too must skills objectives be emphasized in teaching-learning situations. Thus writing for a variety of purposes in science is salient. The science teacher needs to notice if quality attitudes are a by-product of subject matter and skills stressed in the science curriculum. Each pupil is unique in achievement and needs adequate provision so that continuous progress is possible in science. Pertaining to stressing a variety of writing activities in science, Ediger and Rao (1996, pages 86-90) summarized the following:

1. develop an outline. Each pupil with teacher guidance may develop an outline pertaining to content that has been read relating to an ongoing unit of study...
2. develop a written report. The content of the outline may be used to develop a written report. Written reports may deal with—
   (a) summaries of experiments conducted in ongoing units of study in science;

(*b*) diary entries kept by pupils on a daily basis pertaining to understandings, skills, and attitudes acquired. Members on a committee may be rotated in writing these diary entries...

3. write poetry such as haiku, free verse, triplets, and quatrains...
4. other forms of written work such as writing plays announcement, and notices, as well as writing biographies of famous scientists.

A variety of kinds of written work should be emphasized so that pupils learn to communicate clearly and accurately in science.

REFERENCES

American Association for the Advancement of Science (no date given), *Science A Process Approach*. Washington, DC: Ginn and Company.

Ediger, Marlow (1997). *The Modern Elementary School*. Kirksville, Missouri: Simpson Publishing Company, Page 63.

Ediger, Marlow (1996). "The Pupil, Geology, and the Science Curriculum, *School Science*, Vol. 34, No. 34, Page 26.

Ediger, Marlow and D. Bhaskara Rao (1996). *Science Curriculum*. New Delhi, India: Discovery Publishing House, Pages 90-91.

Ediger, Marlow and D. Bhaskara Rao (2000). *Teaching Science Successfully*. New Delhi, India: Discovery Publishing House.

8

Evaluation of Pupil Achievement in Science

There needs to be a variety of approaches used to evaluate pupil achievement in science. Since no approach is perfect, it behooves teachers and supervisors to use diverse methods to determine learner progress in science. Then too, there are numerous facets of a learner's achievement that need to be evaluated making it necessary to use different procedures. These facets include knowledge, skills, and attitudes, among others. We would like to start with discussing teacher observation to appraise pupil achievement.

Teacher Observation of Pupil Progress in Science

Observation by the teacher of each pupil in the classroom during time devoted to teaching science can be rather continuous and ongoing. Perhaps, it is the most common way to evaluate achievement in science teaching and learning. The teacher needs to use quality criteria in appraising pupils in ongoing lessons and units in science. These criteria should include the following:

1. pupils being on task and not digressing from paying attention to ongoing learning activities;
2. pupils being actively involved in identifying and solving problems;

3. pupils developing and testing vital hypotheses in problem solving situations;
4. pupils working harmoniously with others in committee settings and with the class as a whole;
5. pupils making application of what has been learned previously;
6. pupils putting forth optimal effort in individual endeavours;
7. pupils reading science materials with comprehension;
8. pupils writing content clearly and meaningfully in science;
9. pupils evaluating their own achievement in science in a conscientious manner;
10. pupils observing carefully during time devoted to science experiments and demonstrations;
11. pupils speaking accurately and precisely so that quality communication in science takes place.

What has been observed by the teacher may be recorded periodically so that retention of learner achievement is as optimal as possible. One approach in recording pupil achievement is to use anecdotal records. Shepherd and Regan (1982) wrote the following:

Teachers have many opportunities to observe pupils in the classroom, on the playground, in the cafeteria, and in the auditorium. Observations over a period of time in these situations may provide information not revealed in an artificial test situation. For example, pupils may answer yes to a test item. "Do you prefer to work with others rather than by yourself?" When careful observation of their behaviour may reveal that they seldom participate in the activities of a group. Observation also provides an opportunity to report actual behaviour. The pupils who are asked to report on their own behaviours in a formal test situation are likely to give what they perceive to be the expected answer. The report of direct observations is likely, in this instance, to be more reliable than test results. The teacher may also learn a great deal about the personal-social development of children by observing their creative activities. Do the pupils enjoy the activity for its own sake, or do they primarily work for good marks? Do they express their own feelings in their drawings and paintings, or do they prefer to copy the ideas of others?

Anecdotal Records

With anecdotal records, the teacher records learn progress individually at selected intervals. Photocopies may be made to make it convenient in using anecdotal records to record each pupil's achievement. The following form has been used very successfully by teacher whom one of the authors have supervised to record information about a pupil through teacher observation:

Name of Pupil	Date	Observations Made

What might be written, for example, pertaining to pupil's achievement in the classroom, according to teacher observation? The following is provided as an example:

Alex Smyth September 10—Alex worked well with others in the committee to develop a mural on volcanic eruptions. He needed to do more reading and looking at a video so that the opening to the volcano looked more real. Alex seems to enjoy working on the mural with others. He read additional materials on lava and magma, beyond what was discussed in class. Alex enjoys discussing current events items pertaining to volcanic eruptions.

From the above anecdotal record, it appears that Alex tends to do well in science at this point. If a pupil is deficient in an area, the science teacher may then assist the learner in overcoming a difficulty. By looking at the anecdotal record, the teacher may quickly notice what a pupil needs more help in. The teacher may write anecdotal statements on two or three pupils per day so it does not become an overwhelming activity. There must be a purpose in writing anecdotal records and that purpose being to assist pupils to achieve more optimally.

There are other procedures whereby a teacher may observe learner progress and file the results also, in addition to anecdotal records. Journal writing is another procedure for the teacher to use in recording observations made of pupil progress.

Writing Journal Entries

As is true of anecdotal records, journal writing stresses contextual situations of evaluating pupil progress. 'Contextual' means pupils are being evaluated within specific learning activities in terms of observations made by the science teacher to notice what the strengths and weaknesses are of a pupil's progress. Journal entries are written in narrative form, not as precise statements as was true of anecdotal records. The science teacher may focus upon one or two pupils per school day when writing journal entries. It is good to have records of pupil achievement in science. The date for writing in the journal is important. Comparisons might then be made of later with earlier journal entries. A good science teacher is a good evaluator in that he/she knows where each pupil is in achievement and can guide pupils to make continuous progress.

When field studies are being made, pupils need to record comprehensively what was achieved and accomplished. Pertaining to pupils doing field studies in connection with Prince George's Community College, in Largo, Maryland on ospreys and whooping cranes, Cunniff and McMillen (1996) wrote the following:

At the end of the research week, students rank the four research areas in order of preference so that project directors can establish teams to do the data analysis, research presentation, and poster for each area. As expected, working with each species, the ospreys and cranes, is the first choice of many students. However, the project directors are able to place students in their first or second ranked research area. Letting students work in their area of interest promotes a sense of ownership and motivation.

For each research area, the student teams make numerous null and alternative hypotheses. Statistical analysis, done both by hand and computer, is then used to test these hypotheses.

This final week is intense. Each of the four groups analyze the field data along with data from existing databases. Students are graphing software packages to analyze and graph data, test hypotheses, and help reach conclusions. Students develop posters to summarize the research methodology, data analysis, and conclusions. Each team develops a 12 minute presentation, and every student is required to speak. Research presentations are given the Thursday evening of the fourth week to more than 100 persons—parents, teachers, and friends. This activity gives students an opportunity to strengthen communication skills, learn how to give a scientific presentation, use overheads and slides, and work together as a team to deliver a final project, all under a very tight deadline.

There are numerous skills being acquired by pupils in the above named science project; these include doing research, using statistics, reporting orally, and writing observations made.

Using Portfolios to Appraise Pupils Performance

Pupils individually or in committees with teacher guidance need to develop a portfolio to indicate the quality of school work that has been accomplished. Isele (1995) raises questions and provides answers pertaining to portfolio development:

What are student portfolios? A purposeful collection of work that illustrates the student's efforts, progress, and achievement in given areas.

What is the purpose of a student's portfolio? Portfolios provide an ongoing and authentic record of student performance that enable: students to reflect upon and articulate their progress.

Teachers to tailor their instruction to the student's strengths and needs and to use the student's work as a basis for instructional planning. Parents to gain greater insight into their child's learning, administrators/policymakers to base decisions about student achievement on authentic and meaningful information.

What are benefits of portfolios? Portfolios

- portray students' processes as well as products;
- involve students in reflecting upon their learning, and thereby, provide individual responsibility, self-sufficiency, and active involvement;
- increase time spent on learning and the quality of teaching;
- provide a tangible and meaningful basis for discussions among students, teachers, and parents;
- link curriculum, instruction, and assessment;
- inform instruction.

Portfolios have a rather recent history in their use to appraise pupil achievement. We have observed portfolios to be wisely used by student teachers and cooperating teachers whom we have supervised in the public schools. What should go into a portfolio containing products of pupil achievement in science?

1. snapshots and videos of pupils working on science experiments;
2. cassette recordings of pupils working on committees in collaborative endeavours;
3. art products and written work of the pupil in ongoing lessons and units of study in science;
4. diary entries kept by the learner on a daily basis and dated pertaining to what was learned in science. Written products may come from word processor use;
5. log entries which summarize the diary entries;
6. pupil summaries of major concepts and generalizations acquired in science units of study;

7. descriptions of pupil/teacher conferences covering a science unit of study;
8. self evaluation by the pupil on strengths acquired during the entire unit of study. The pupil may wish to list what areas he/she needs more assistance in;
9. results from teacher written, standardized tests, as well as norm referenced tests;
10. a listing of computer packages completed. Internet may well be used to obtain information in problem solving experiences. A table of contents should be developed for the portfolio.

Collins and Dana (1993) suggest that four kinds of data or evidence be in a portfolio; these are the following:

1. artefacts are documents normally created or used in schools such as tests, book reports, work sheets, projects, etc.;
2. reproductions are items that typify events of activities in which students normally engage but often are not captured. For example, audio/visual taped discussions, presentations or photographs of projects or other work;
3. attestations often take the form of a letter prepared by someone other than the student verifying his/her work or contributions;
4. productions take two forms, both of which are especially created for the portfolio. The first is a reflective entry which articulates what was learned from the project or activity. The second is a caption affixed to each portfolio entry describing what it is and why it is included.

Pupils with teacher guidance need to have definite categories in mind when having the former develop a portfolio. These identified categories assist the learner in thinking about how to organise the portfolio and its contents. A wide variety of processes and products should be in evidence in a portfolio. Interested, responsible persons, especially parents, may then see what the learner has accomplished and what needs to be worked on to further the progress of the pupil.

After appraising diverse procedures used to evaluate pupil achievement. Ediger (1995) wrote:

Approaches used to appraise pupil progress depend upon the philosophy of education involved. Each specific philosophy has uniqueness attached in determining that which learners have acquired.

The testing and measurement movement stresses the utilization of predetermined objectives written in measurable terms. The objectives are written prior to instruction of learners. With appropriate learning opportunities, either a pupil does or does not achieve one or more precise objectives. Measuring pupil progress against the stated objectives emphasizes the concept of criterion referenced testing (CRT).

The testing and measurement movement also advocates using norm referenced tests (NRT). Pupils are spread out on a continuum from highest to lowest based on test scores. Predetermined objectives tend not to exist when utilizing norm referenced tests to measure pupil achievement. Norm referenced tests spread pupils' results in terms of test scores much more so than criterion referenced testing. Pupils attempt to attain predetermined objectives with CRTs. The measurably stated objectives represent absolute standards. A high number of pupils might well achieve the measurably stated objectives, as the teacher usually intends.

Self evaluation by the pupil is an opposite approach to appraisal of learner progress as contrasted with the testing and measurement movement. With self evaluation, the responsibility rests upon the learner himself/herself to acknowledge strengths, weaknesses, and modifications to attain at a higher level. Learners when evaluating the self need to perceive the processes and products completed from the frame of reference of personal improvement. Truth, in results from the evaluation, may well reside within the pupil. Subjectivity in results is to be expected, since open-ended criteria are utilized to appraise progress. With self evaluation, the pupil might well perceive increased purpose in assessing the self. The teacher is a stimulator and initiator when guiding the self evaluation process.

Testing to Determine Pupils Achievement

Using tests as a sole determiner to ascertain pupil achievement has lost its popularity and luster than what it once had. However, test results can still provide the teacher with feedback pertaining to a pupil's achievement. Testing occurs in a noncontextual situation and thus does not have the utilitarian features that a contextual situation has. For example, if a pupil writes a "thank you notice" to a person or place where the classroom took an excursion, the situation is practical and the letter will be mailed to the proper destination. The involved letter of appreciation was written in context in a life like situation. Tests taken by pupils are outside the framework of a utilitarian situation. People in society then do not take tests to show how well they are doing their work. Rather they are appraised in terms of how well they perform at the work place. An automobile mechanic might then be appraised in terms of how few complaints are received from customers as to faulty work having been done on their cars and trucks. The carpenter on the job does not take a paper/ pencil tests to show how well he/she did in building a home or other structure. Instead, the carpenter reveals proficiency by his/her skills and abilities to build a cabinet in the house, shingle the roof of the dwelling, and lay tiles for the basement floor, among other needed tasks.

To use the same analogy, the pupil in school has purposes for writing such as writing a "get well notice" to a friend who is ill, inviting friends to a birthday party, sending a thank you notice for a gift or favour received, and/or corresponding with pen pals. Here, the pupil is not evaluated in letter writing through a paper pencil test using multiple choice test items. In context, the pupil should be appraised in how well he/she writes, not how well a test can be taken. The term 'constructivism' is also given to appraising pupil achievement in writing within a contextual situation. The contextual situation stresses practical and utilitarian situations. Knowledge and skills are put to use. Application is then made of knowledge and skills possessed by the learner.

Now getting back to testing of pupils in the curriculum, should testing be avoided? We think not. Why? Testing is one method of appraising pupil achievement. The teacher when writing these tests items needs to use quality standards. Subject matter contained should be valid for the test. In other words, the teacher in teaching and learning situations has covered the content written as test items, generally multiple choice in nature. The teacher needs to be certain that the test items are clearly written; ambiguity has been omitted. The stem of the multiple choice item is grammatically correct with each of the four distracters. The following is given as an example:

Reptiles have all but one of the following characteristics:

(a) temperature readings are comparable to that of the environment;

(b) their live are born from eggs that have hatched;

(c) babies are very dependent upon adults for at least a month;

(d) in their phylum are animals such as turtles, snakes, and alligators.

The responses should be quite similar in length when writing multiple choice items so that clues are not available to the pupil as to which the correct answer would be. It is much easier to write multiple choice items measuring factual responses as compared to higher levels of cognition.

Many teachers write true-false items to measure pupil achievement. If a test item here is false, pupils should correct what is incorrect so that a minimal amount of guessing is involved. In the following true-false item, the pupil needs to correct what is false:

First start their lives breathing through the use of gills and later develop lungs.

There are teachers who write matching test items to measure pupil achievement in science. What is matched is usually factual in nature. There are important facts for pupils to understand in science. To match column A with column B, there needs to be more items in one column as compared to the next so that the process of elimination may not be used excessively. There should not be more than ten items in one column for intermediate grade levels. One column in the matching test should have single words of phrases; it is difficult to match column A with column B if both have lengthy sentences.

Teacher written test items should possess reliability. Thus if a test is taken a second time by the same set of learners, the results would be similar from one testing time to the next for individual learners. Should these test results vary much for one child from one testing to the next using the same items, the test would lack reliability. It would not too be useful to notice where a pupil is, on the same test, if on the first testing, John has 90 per cent right and for the second testing 30 per cent correct. The question would then arise as to where is John in achievement since the scores vary much on the same test from one testing to the next. There are basically three kinds of reliability statistically. These are test-retest, split half, and alternate forms.

Teacher written tests are one kind to be taken by pupils. Generally teachers align their tests with what has been taught. Thus, there are degrees of validity there.

There appear to be weaknesses no matter which procedure is used in testing. Thus, in standardized testing, teachers have no objectives to go by to know which subject matter will be covered in the test. The manual section will say how the items were selected to be on the standardized test. But, it leaves the science teacher in a precarious situation in terms of having some guidance as to what pupils should learn in ongoing science units of study in order to do well on the standardized instrument. Quality standardized tests will contain in the manual section the validity and reliability figures from schools having used these tests. Reliability figures given are high since it is relatively easy to develop quality reliability figures when spending a considerable amount of money to secure needed test-retest, alternative forms, and/or split-half reliability. It is much more difficult to obtain quality 'validity' for the standardized test. The science teacher should have statements of clearly stated objectives so that he/she may teach in a manner which will assist pupils to achieve desired objectives. The learning activities in science would then be valid for the stated objectives. Otherwise, the teacher would be uncertain in knowing what to teach so that pupils do well on the test.

A publishing company of standardized tests has specific rules to follow, indicated in the manual, as to how to administer the test. Each pupil taking the test follows the same rules and has the same time limits. Thus there are standard procedure in test taking. To score the tests, the same key is used for all pupils and with machine scoring, no errors should be made in checking each pupil's paper. Test results, if checked again, should be the same for each pupil no matter who or what scores the tests.

From pupil results, there should be quite a range from high to low in pupils' test scores in anyone grade level. The standardized tests are constructed in ways which make it possible to have this wide spread of scores.

Criterion referenced tests have taken some of the weaknesses out of standardized testing. Here, teachers have statements of objectives to use in teaching science. The teacher needs to choose learning opportunities in order that learners may attain the objectives. Thus the learning opportunities harmonize with the stated objectives and provide for validity.

The testing device also aligns with the stated objectives, thus making for validity in testing. Ideally, there should be a small range in pupils' test scores from a criterion referenced test. Why? The science teacher teaches so that as many pupils as possible achieve the stated objectives. Thus, it can be expected that the range of scores from high to low on criterion referenced tests will be much more marginal as compared to standardized tests.

There are numerous states that mandate criterion referenced tests for pupils to take on selected grade levels. Accountability of teachers may be tied in with criterion referenced testing. Thus, teachers are held accountable for pupils achieving the precise objectives whose subject matter is being measured on the criterion referenced test.

There is considerable debate presently as to how much should test results count as compared to portfolio content in appraising pupil achievement. Tests possess much subjectivity when subject matter is selected for inclusion. There certainly would not be agreement on which science content should go into a test. Objectivity occurs here when the results from pupil testing is being evaluated. If the results are scored accurately, there should be no subjectivity involved providing all scorers use the same scoring key. With portfolios, subjectivity is involved when two or three raters appraise any one portfolio. It will be difficult for these raters to come up with the same results when evaluating each person's progress. Kane and Khaturi (1995) wrote the following:

Some questions related to performance assessment remain to be answered by future research. They have to do with basic and secondary issues in educational reform... What knowledge and skills are pupils to demonstrate after a certain period of schooling? What other systemic reforms must be undertaken in order for assessment reforms to be effective? What assessment formats are most useful for which specific purposes? The greatest challenge ahead lies in designing systems of reform that synergistically support the core educational functions of teaching and learning for which teachers are the most powerful 'engine'.

Conferences with Pupils

The conference method can be an excellent way of assisting the teacher to determine what pupils have learned in science. Ediger (1996) wrote:

The teacher may conduct conferences with pupils individually or in a group setting. If a pupil, for example, has completed reading a library book directly related to the ongoing unit of study, the teacher may conduct an informal conference to determine attitudes and comprehension of the involved learner. The teacher might also conduct a conference with a small group of pupils who have read the same or related library books. Thus, learners may read library books on the following topics relating to the present unit being studied in science:

1. The seasons, plants, and animals.
2. Plants and animals of prehistoric times.
3. The uses of nuclear energy.
4. Uses of magnets and electricity.
5. Constellations and the universe.

Pupils may reveal learnings such as the following in a conference setting pertaining to content gained from reading selected library books:

1. obtaining skills in reading critically and creatively;
2. acquiring selected facts, main ideas, and generalizations,
3. selecting ideas which come in a certain sequence;
4. reading to solve problems;
5. wishing to engage in reading for recreational purposes.

Conference methods of evaluating pupil achievement may be used along with other appraisal procedures. A conference may take a very short period of teacher time. Other may take longer depending upon the agenda of the science teacher. We believe conferences are a marvellous way of getting to know pupils better as individuals as well as guiding learners to achieve more optimally. In conferences with pupils as well as with any facet of the science curriculum. We believe teachers need to think about four questions pertaining to science lessons and units of study that Ralph Tyler (1949) raised:

1. Which objectives should pupils achieve?
2. Which learning activities should be chosen to assist pupils to achieve the stated objectives?
3. How should these learning activities be organised?
4. How should we evaluate to know if the objective have been achieved?

These four questions might well provide for a framework for planning and implementing a quality science curriculum.

Discussions and Pupil Achievement

Pupils with teacher leadership should have ample opportunities to discuss content acquired in science. Learners need to understand and attach meaning to what has been learned. Rote learning and memorization of subject matter is not adequate. Pupils also need to comprehend and use what has been learned. Discussions can be lively and engaging. They certainly do not need to be dull. We have observed teachers lead discussions in classrooms whereby each pupil was truly involved wholeheartedly. In discussions seem to be boring and lead nowhere, pupils with teacher assistance need to determine causes for these occurrences. Science is a fascinating curriculum area in which pupils may truly ponder over questions and problems as well as being actively involved in each learning opportunity. Pertaining to discussions, Ediger (1977) wrote the following:

In discussion settings, feedback from learners is obtained in terms of relevant concepts and generalizations gained in a specific unit of study. Thus, learners may reveal the following understandings in a discussion:

1. What causes earthquakes, cyclones, and hurricanes.
2. What causes diverse kinds of weather on the earth's surface.
3. How gasoline and electrical engines operate in terms of involved scientific principles.

Using discussions as a technique to appraise learner progress, pupils also indicate

1. if they can stay on the topic being pursued;
2. if they can communicate ideas orally in an effective manner;
3. if they respect the thinking of others.

By listening to oral reports given by pupils, the teacher may notice learner growth in the following ways:

1. Has the report been carefully planned and prepared?
2. Is there appropriate sequence of content being presented?
3. Does the reporter really understand the content being presented to listeners? Thus if a pupil is reporting on cirrus clouds, does he/she understand how these clouds are formed as well as have accurate perceptions on their physical appearances?
4. Does the learner speak clearly enough so listeners can clearly understand the contents being presented?

There should be ample time given after the oral report for listeners to ask questions and make comments in an atmosphere of respect. It is very important for pupils to learn to accept and respect each other. In an atmosphere of acceptance and belonging, pupils probably will learn more subject matter content than would otherwise be the case.

Conclusion

The development and use of portfolios should be a way for pupils to reflect upon their strengths and weaknesses in working toward higher achievement levels. Bimes-Michalak (1995) believes that a major reason for developing portfolios is for pupils and teachers to reflect upon what has been taught and learned. There is a motivating ingredient in portfolio development and that is active involvement by learners in compiling a truly excellent device to inform others of personal progress in science. The pupil is involved in a hands on approach in determining what should go into a portfolio and why. Gilman and Rafferty (no date given) list the following advantages of using portfolios to appraise pupil achievement:

1. they evaluate both process and product;
2. they allow an integration of learning and assessment;
3. evaluation is not limited to a single score;
4. provide more information about a student's progress;
5. they encourage students to take charge of their own learning;
6. students feel they are a part of the assessment process;
7. they help develop the skills for lifelong learning;
8. they may actually reduce the daily burden of grading papers;
9. the information gained from portfolios is meaningful and substantial;
10. they provide a continuous example of a child's work in a context that is relevant and understandable;
11. they assess global understanding and thinking skills;
12. it is a form of evaluation that is bound to have parental approval.

Wolf (1996) suggests teachers also develop their own portfolios. He wrote the following:

Why this interest in portfolios? Although portfolios can be time consuming to construct and cumbersome to review, they also capture the complexities of professional practices in ways that no other approach can. Not only are they an effective way to assess teaching quality, but they also provide teachers opportunities for self reflection and collegial interactions based on documented episodes of their own teaching.

Essentially, a teaching portfolio is a collection of information such as lesson plans, student assignments, teacher's written descriptions and videotapes of their instruction, and formal evaluations by supervisors...

Teachers and administrators need to look for better means of evaluation of pupil progress than what was used previously. Changes need to be made when moving from *what is* to *what should be*. What should be is based on the best thinking possible in education. Using test scores largely to reveal learner progress and achievement was weighted and found wanting. Norm and criterion referenced tests provided some data on pupil achievement, but the scope was very narrow in showing what a pupil knows and can do. Test results show numerical data scores, such as norm referenced results indicating how well a pupil compares with others in taking the same test. Percentile ranks, standard deviations, grade equivalents, and quartile deviations are given to show how well a pupil is doing in the curriculum. Or in the case of criterion referenced tests, information is given if a pupil has or has not achieved predetermined objectives. Numerical test results do not indicate how well a person communicates orally or in writing in a contextual situation. The tests also are taken outside the framework of the ongoing lesson or unit of study being presented. Pupils then lack ownership of indicating how well they are doing in the curriculum area of science.

REFERENCES

Bimes-Michalak, Beverly (1995), "The Portfolio Zone," *Education Digest*. 60: 53-57.

Collins, A., and T.M. Dana (1993), "Using Portfolios with Middle Grade Students," *Middle School Journal*, 25: 14-19.

Cuniff, Patricia A., and Janet L. McMillen (1996), "Field Studies," *The Science Teacher*, 63: 51.

Ediger, Marlow (1995). *Philosophy in Curriculum Development*. Kirksville, Missouri: Simpson Publishing Company, Pages 114-115.

Ediger, Marlow (1996). *Elementary Education (A Collection of Essays)*. Kirksville, Missouri; Simpson Publishing Company, Page 149.

Ediger, Marlow (1977). *The Elementary Curriculum. A Handbook*. Kirksville, Missouri: Simpson Publishing Company, Pages 215-216.

Gilman, David Alan, and Cathleen D, D. Rafferty. (no date given). "Portfolios: They're Just Not Work Folders Anymore," School of Education, Indiana State University, Terre Haute: Curriculum and Research Center.

Isele, Frederick (1995), "Performance Based Portfolios." Paper presented at the National Council Social Studies Convention, Chicago.

Kane, Michael, and Nidh Khatri (1995), "Assessment Reform," *Phi Delta Kappan*, 77:32.

Shepherd, Gene D., and William B. Ragan. *Modern Elementary Curriculum*. New York: Holt, Rinehart and Winston, Pages 109-110.

Tylor, Ralph (1949). *Basic Principles of Curriculum and Instruction*. Chicago: University of Chicago Press.

Wolf, Kenneth (1996), "Developing an Effective Teaching Portfolio," *Educational Leadership*, 53:34.

9

Cooperative Learning Versus Competition in Science

Most educators appear to advocate cooperative learning in the curriculum. Pupils then are to work together harmoniously to achieve objectives in the curriculum. Heterogeneous grouping is also recommended so that mixed achievement levels of pupil work in a committee setting. These educators emphasize democratic living in the classroom when pupils are grouped heterogeneously as compared to homogeneously. Cooperative endeavours stresses democracy as a way of life, according to many educators, as compared to competition among pupils in the classroom. If full inclusion is emphasized, then a committee in cooperative learning may truly be heterogeneous with increased diversity in terms of pupils abilities. Let us examine the philosophy of cooperative learning and heterogeneous grouping more fully.

Cooperative Learning

As we read journal articles and other teacher education materials, we feel that most educators advocate cooperative learning throughout much of the school day. There is a distinctive kind of reasoning emphasized by advocates. Pupils may then learn from each other. Perhaps, more can be learned from peers as compared to the teacher. Learners are cooperative beings and like to work together with other pupils. Cooperative learning can be emphasized in all curriculum areas and throughout most or all of the school day. Pupils are serious achievers when working together with peers. Each one desires to do his/her fair share of work within a committee. Fast learners can assist the slower pupils to achieve well. They can learn from the slow learners in return. Pupils need to learn to get along with each other and to respect the abilities of others. Diversity in the curriculum is to be stressed.

We believe there are numerous loopholes in the reasoning of cooperative learning advocates. We emphasize that not all pupils by any means are cooperative. There is rivalry, hostility, and aggression among pupils. To be sure, there are many pupils who are cooperative beings in wishing to work well together with others in an harmonious manner. One has only to observe pupil behaviour to notice that pupils are both cooperative and noncooperative beings. We thoroughly agree that pupils should learn to work well with others in school and later in the work place. But to what degree in terms of the total length of the school day should pupils work on cooperative endeavours. Our thinking is that pupils should work in committees effectively since life itself consists of working well with others. However, there are many times when individuals need to work by the self. All of us find ourselves working on tasks and responsibilities by the oneself, without involvement of others. Thus there needs to a rational balance in the school curriculum between working with others as well as working individually on tasks and activities.

There is seemingly a learning style which pupils possess that prefers working with others on lessons, projects and activities. These pupils, no doubt, might well prefer a committee or cooperative learning experience. Together, the pupil may achieve more than working individually. These pupils might be motivated more so with other learners than working by the self. Learners may motivate and challenge each other in a committee setting and yet efforts are harmonized to attain a togetherness in an educational endeavour. Pupils need to be highly accepting of each other in cooperative learning. They must respect diversity among pupils and ideas. The use of ridicule and sarcasm is to be frowned upon. Rather, the pupil needs to encourage broad participation by members of the team. Group cohesion is necessary so that the goals of cooperative learning are being attained. The committee may be evaluated together as well as individually in their team contributions. All need to participate actively and achieve maximally. Failure for one or two to achieve in cooperative learning hinders optimal attainment for these pupils. Each must be serious in preserving and working toward objectives. The individual needs to blend his/her efforts with those of others on the team. All on the team must participate optimally, no one dominate the committee endeavours. Learners should stay on the task at hand, not digress from agreed upon goals. Tasks need to become clear through interacting with each other. Achievement toward goals must be reviewed periodically in order to notice how much progress has been made and how much further the committee needs to go in order to achieve agreed upon goals.

The teacher in cooperative learning becomes a guide, a stimulator, and one who encourages, but not one who lectures not dispenses information. He/she is a resource person who has much knowledge of keeping pupils on task. The teacher as resource person has numerous materials and necessary information from which pupils in cooperative learning may gather what is needed to achieve objectives. As a helper and facilitator, the teacher is motivated to assist pupils to be creative, to engage in critical thought, and to identify and solve problems. Higher levels of cognition are necessary here. The teacher knows how to relate to learners in order that higher levels of cognition on the pupil's part in teaching and learning is in evidence.

There are selected questions that need to be raised pertaining to cooperative learning. These are the following:

1. How much time in the school day should be given to cooperative learning?

2. How should committees be formed for cooperative learning?
3. Who selects members of a committee?
4. How permanent should committee membership be?
5. How flexible should committee membership be if a pupil wishes to change to a different committee?

Frequently, one of the authors have received the impression that writers/speakers in education recommend continuous cooperative endeavours in a classroom. Certainly, learning opportunities need to be varied. Little is mentioned as to who should choose committee members. The teacher may make the choice. Pupils could also volunteer to serve on a committee. Random selection could be used to determine committee membership. Committee membership could be very short indeed for a particular group, perhaps a day or several days. Membership could be rather enduring also, such as planned tasks that last six weeks or so. There are different types of tasks such as those that are short in duration, such as planning refreshments for an end of the school year party. Cooperative learning members could also be together for an entire thematic unit of six weeks such as planning and making a model bedouin village in a unit on The Middle East. There will be pupils who do not like the project or a selected pupil on the committee. What is the answer here? This happens even if members have been chosen carefully using desired criteria.

Competition in the School Curriculum

There are a few educators, not many, who advocate a competitive curriculum. Many reasons are given for the competitive philosophy. Generally, it is based upon the free enterprise system. Advocates believe with competition, bad schools and teachers will have no clients and therefore not be in existence. The better schools with more clients than ever will serve as models for other teachers to emulate. Competition for numbers of pupils in a school is strictly competitive. Poor schools will go out of business.

Merit pay has numerous advocates. With merit pay teachers rated as being superior or excellent receive additional pay for their quality services. Those supporting merit pay believe that teachers individually will work harder and do a better job of teaching once they are rewarded for doing outstanding work. Differentiated pay is then desired among teachers. No longer would the single salary schedule then be in operation. The latter is based on the number of years of teaching experience and the level of attained education at colleges/universities as being sole determines of salary to be obtained by a teacher. Critics state that mediocrity is rewarded in teaching with the single salary schedule. If merit pay is implemented, competition for the higher salaries would then definitely be in evidence.

Open enrolment also emphasizes the free enterprise system. Here, parents choose for their sons and daughters which kind of a school the latter are to attend. The chosen school may bypass many local schools and school systems. Parents and the child do the choosing not the local school or the locally assigned teacher. The purpose is competition in parents choosing which school and teacher is best for their offspring. Teachers and schools not selected may need statewide superintendents and newly retrained and re-educated teachers.

The Secretary of Education may list state by state how well pupils are achieving in different curriculum areas. This is called the wall chart. States are compared against each other in terms of pupil achievement, money spent on education per pupil, and average daily attendance of pupils. With competition among the different states in terms of wall chart figures, personal pride of each state to improve in education might be an end result when making these comparisons, according to selected educators and many lay people.

There are schools that have arranged contracts with commercial companies to teach their children. Educational Alternatives Incorporated (EAI) from Minneapolis, Minnesota is an example. EAI agrees with the school district how much achievement and the cost of services will be involved in a given school year. EAI then assumes responsibility for administration and instruction of the involved schools. There is competition here between the public schools and commercial companies in terms of who can provide the best education for pupils. It might well be true that school administrators and teachers remain the same with EAI as compared to earlier arrangements. EAI still does the training of teachers to use methodology as they deem to be good and profitable.

Additional means of competing with the public schools in terms of teaching pupils is to have charter schools and magnet schools.

When supervising student and cooperating teachers in the schools. We have observed the following to encourage competition among pupils in the classroom setting:

1. a chart on the wall showing the names of each pupil in class indicating how many words were spelled correctly for each week using the basal spelling text. Gold stars were received by the top spellers, followed by silver stars for the next best set of spellers. Other colours of stars were situated next to the name of the pupil indicating his/her spelling achievement;
2. the teacher announcing to the entire class how many problems each pupil solved correctly from one lesson from the basal text in mathematics. The announcements were made for each day of pupil practice in mathematics using the basal textbook;
3. pupil test results in social studies were posted on the bulletin board ranking learners from high to low in achievement. The teacher commented on how well or how poorly individual pupils here had achieved;
4. prizes announced prior to beginning a new unit in science. These prizes were to be awarded to pupils depending upon how many total points each received as a result of participating in different projects and tasks;

5. the pupil of the day selected by the teacher being presented with and wearing 'the king's or queen's hat. There was much competition among pupils in class in being able to wear this hat for a day.

There are many additional examples which can be given whereby competition can and is being emphasized in the classroom setting. Pupils are compared with each other as to term projects, daily assignments, oral reports, oral reading, and test results, among other items. A major purpose of standardized tests is to compare one pupil against another. A parent, after receiving information of test results from his/her offspring, may during informal conversation, compare test results with parents of other children. We have heard parents reprimand their children for not doing better on a standardized test. Generally, the reprimand emphasizes why the child did not do better than so and so. Many parents are highly competitive in wanting their offspring to be a cheer leader, member of the first team in football or basketball, have a leading role in the school play, and/or being a class officer.

Competition can be healthy; it can also be destructive.

Cooperative learning can be positive as well as negative. It all depends upon what transpires in either competitive or cooperative situations.

We will first discuss healthy competition. Here, pupils respect each other even though one or more persons in a given situation do not experience victory. Healthy competition can bring out the best within the person. Effort and perseverance is involved! There can be much interest on the part of all in competition be it between individuals or within a committee competing against another committee. We recommend the following guidelines for stressing competitive events:

1. those competing should be somewhat equivalent in talents, skills, and abilities;
2. those competing should have positive attitudes toward each other;

3. those competing should have a desire to participate and learn;
4. those competing should have definite goals to achieve in the competitive event;
5. those competing should realize that not all individuals can be winners. Best it is if all pupils can be winners! This is definitely possible.

Questions that might be raised about competitive behaviour in the classroom setting include the following:

1. Does competition increase hostility among pupils toward each other?
2. Does competition hinder pupils in achieving affective objectives?
3. Does competition work against the learning style of selected pupils?
4. Does competition compare involved pupils unfavourable due to differences in abilities, interests, and capabilities?
5. Does competition increase achievement of pupils?

Teachers might wish to encourage positive competition among individuals in the classroom setting. Competition is neither good nor bad, but it depends upon how it affects individuals.

We all need to realize that as adults, we compete in numerous ways such as for jobs and occupations, promotions, marriage partners, good grades in classes taken, and for leadership responsibilities in society, among others.

Cooperative learning has its advantages and disadvantages. The advantages are the following:

1. pupils do have opportunities here in learning to work together with others;
2. selected pupils have as their favourite learning style the working together with peers, rather than working individually;

3. goals in life can be achieved in cooperating with each other, rather than through dog eat dog approaches;
4. learners can realize that school and learning may be enjoyable through cooperative learning;
5. pupils need to learn to assist each other in the school and classroom setting. We human beings are dependent upon each other for survival.

Questions which need to be raised about cooperative learning include the following:

1. Might pupils become highly competitive in a negative way within a committee setting?
2. Might personality clashes hinder pupil achievement in committee settings?
3. Might there be learning styles whereby selected pupils do not do well in group work, but would achieve better in more competitive settings? We would like to emphasize here that pupils individually may compete against their past performance with intent of making continuous progress?
4. Might there be a rational balance between individual and committee endeavours in the curriculum which could benefit most pupils?
5. Might there be leaders who do their best in cooperative learning?

There are no clear cut answers to these questions. Even well designed research studies have their many weakness. Human beings write test items for the measurement device, ensuring much subjectivity in a research study. Objectivity occurs when all conditions are kept similar in giving the tests to the experimental and the control groups. Or can they be similar/same? No, they are not. Pupils feel differently from one time to the next. Not all pupils find that revealing what has been learned occurs best through testing. There are pupils who like authentic means of revealing what has been learned better as compared to being tested.

In Closing

Educators need to re-examine the cooperation versus competition philosophies in teaching pupils. Which approach is better of the two? It is hard to say. Neither approach in and of itself is good. There can be negative teaching in either approach. We have seen bad teaching as well as good teaching in either case. Merely having cooperative learning or saying that one has cooperative learning does not make for goodness or badness. What truly matters is how each approach affects learners in the school and classroom setting. We would recommend having rational balance among the two approaches. Pupils need to learn to work harmoniously with others as well as work well on an individual basis. Each pupil should strive to achieve optimally when working individually. After all, life in school and in society consists of both!

10

Outputs, Inputs, and the Science Teacher

Numerous speakers and writers in education talk about the desirability of outputs from pupils largely or only. Thus test results from pupils which show good achievement are wanted. Inputs, according to these speakers and writers, are of secondary or minimal importance. Let us analyze the advocacy of outputs with minimal attention paid to inputs.

Test Results and Outputs

Test results appear to be objective to many. They provide numerical data to show learner achievement. A pupil, for example, is on the fiftieth percentile on results from a standardized or norm referenced test. Or, a pupil is one standard deviation above the mean according to test results. Further ways of expressing pupil results from testing would be to say a pupil is working on the 6.2 grade equivalent or is on stanine five.

A realist in educational philosophy desires to have preciseness in stating where a pupil is in academic achievement. Much emphasis is placed upon validity in that tests should measure what they purport to measure, such as academic achievement or personal-social adjustment. Consistency of results be it split-half, alternative forms, or test-retest approaches are needed to indicate reliability. Correlational results in numerical terms are needed to show degrees of correlation in validity and reliability. Correlations then show the strength of relationships between two or more variables, such as the strength or relationship between two achievement tests or two IQ tests.

Measuring pupil progress, according to realists, becomes the major or only way of ascertaining pupil progress. Measurably stated objectives are advocated in that pupils reveal if they have/have not attained any one objective. A yes or no situation is involved here. Precision is needed to show how well a pupil is doing in school. Behaviourism as a psychology of learning is being emphasized. Teaching toward ends becomes a major goal of the teacher. The ends are the measurably stated objectives for pupils to attain. Testing is necessary to reveal if a pupil is successful in goal attainment. Numerical results are in the offing which communicate clearly to parents how well an offspring is doing in school. Stress then is placed on outcomes from the learner, inputs become relatively unimportant.

Standardized norm referenced achievement tests do not have related predetermined measurably stated objectives for pupils to achieve whereas criterion referenced tests do. Thus for criterion referenced tests, a teacher may announce to pupils, prior to instruction, what they are to learn from the teaching and learning act. This provides security to learners in that they now know what is expected of them in terms of achievement or outputs.

Communication with parents becomes easier when a precise numeral can be given pertaining to the offspring's achievement. It is also easier in the accountability movement to hold teachers accountable for learners attaining that which is stated in the predetermined objectives. These objectives are usually developed on the state or district level. By having access to the measurably stated objectives, prior to instruction, the teacher selects learning opportunities so that learners may achieve the measurably stated objectives. With the related criterion referenced tests, the teacher measures if pupils are or are not doing satisfactory work. Validity is in evidence if the criterion referenced tests measure that which is stated in the measurable objectives. Reliability is present if pupils tend to receive consistent results in and on the same test be it test-retest, split-half, and/or alternative forms of reliability.

To every action, there appears to be an opposite and equal reaction, a law of physics, which appears to be true in methods of determining pupil achievement. Among others, the following are weaknesses of using measuring procedures only, to determine learner achievement:

1. the test results are not objective in that human beings wrote the test items for both norm and criterion referenced tests. Human beings choosing what goes into a test in terms of content in test items emphasizes a bias and subjective thinking;
2. 'objectivity' is brought in after the test items have been tried out on learners in pilot studies to develop numerical results, such as percentile ranks, standard deviation scores, stanines, and correlations, among others;
3. 'objective' test items are limited as to what can be measured. Too frequently critical and creative thinking, as well as problem solving are omitted from norm and criterion referenced tests. These processes are difficult to measure numerically;
4. tests are external to the teaching and learning situation. They do not measure what is contextual or that which is sequential in learning opportunities. Norm and criterion referenced tests are developed by those who are outside of the local classroom in which pupils are tested as well as outside the framework where teaching and learning occurred;
5. tests cannot measure such items as quality oral communication, skill in construction experiences or experimentation, among others. They are very weak in measuring personality and social traits of pupils.

A further major weakness pertains to educators and lay people believing that the ends only count in terms of pupils achievement. Accountability of teachers then is related to how well pupils do on tests, regardless of ability levels or socioeconomic statuses of the learner. Little stress then needs to be given to inputs or means to an end. The ends are the precisely stated objective(s). How can quality instruction occur unless there are adequate materials of instruction to use so that the objectives may be achieved by learners?

We recommend that adequate attention be given to inputs so that any teacher has adequate materials of instruction to use in teaching. Pupils might attain as optimally as possible when interacting with quality materials of instruction.

Experimentalism in Teaching

Experimentalism as a philosophy of education advocates that one can only know experience, not the real world as it truly is. To experience means to interact with the natural and social environment. Thus the teacher needs to have adequate learning opportunities so that pupils might have rich experiences in the curriculum. These experiences need to be lifelike and real, not rote learning and memorization. The teacher here needs to provide a variety of realistic activities which assist pupils to attain vital goals of instruction. What is this vital goal or goals?

Experimentalists realize that change is all around us. We experience change, not sameness nor consistent stability. With continuous change, problems arise which need solutions. The world is no longer the same but has modifications. These modifications or changes make for the necessity of identification of relevant problems. Thus the pupil with teacher guidance needs to select relevant problems. The ultimate goal of instruction then is to have pupils engage in problem solving experiences. The problems are selected in context, not in isolation from the ongoing unit of study. There are subsidiary flexible objectives inherent in problem solving. Thus in addition to the selection of relevant problems (a subsidiary objective), the pupil needs to learn to develop a hypothesis which is a tentative answer to the problem (subsidiary objective two). The hypothesis needs to be tested in a lifelike situation (subsidiary objective number three). A fourth flexible subsidiary objective for the pupil to attain is to revise the hypothesize if necessary. Problem solving here stresses the complete act of thought. Time is necessary for pupils to be engaged in problem solving activities. The teacher stimulates, challenges, and encourages pupils to achieve, grow, and develop.

With problem solving, pupils need to interact with materials that relate to reality, the social and natural environment. Predetermined objectives do not harmonize with experimentalism and problem solving. The teacher then cannot state predetermined problems for pupils to solve unless learners accept these as their very own. Otherwise, pupils should identify problems in context in ongoing lessons and units of study. The complete act of thought or problem solving procedures need to be stressed.

Which activities should be available to assist pupils in problem solving? A multimedia approach should be used. Concrete (excursions, objects, realia, construction endeavours, creative and formal dramatics and models, among others), semiconcrete (video disks, cassette tapes with accompanying filmstrips, slides, video tapes, among others), and abstract learning opportunities (computers and accompanying software, radio, cassette tapes, oral and silent reading of content, internet and resource personnel, among others) should be in the offing to solve problems.

An experience centred curriculum requires many materials of instruction. Ends or objectives to achieve emphasize problem solving by pupils with teacher guidance. The cost of inputs will be relatively high since there needs to be subject matter available from multimedia to solve problems. The outputs are also important in that pupils need to identify and solve relevant problems relating school and society which become one, not separate entities. Numerical results of pupil achievement is not feasible nor possible.

Experimentalists advocate that pupils work in committees to solve problems since in the societal arenas, collaboration is emphasized to choose and solve problems.

Existentialism and the Curriculum

A third philosophy of education to implement is existentialism. Existentialists are strong in pupils making decisions to the maximum extent possible. Decision making by learners is of utmost importance. A learning stations approach may be implemented. An adequate number of stations need to be in evidence so that pupils may choose which tasks to complete at different stations. Each station has concrete, semiconcrete, and abstract materials of instruction for pupils. The tasks are printed on small cards at each station. The learner may then select sequential tasks to complete. With an ample number of tasks at each station, the pupil may omit those not possessing perceived purpose. Cooperative learning or individual endeavours may be chosen; the tasks selected may or may not stress problem solving. Existentialists tend to emphasize tasks for learner choice which reflect the human dimension. Thus learning activities reflect content pertaining to the tensions and anxieties that individuals experience in life every day.

The individual pupil should do the choosing of tasks to pursue, not the committee or group, unless the pupil chooses to engage in group work. Tasks at the different stations should have those that stress individual as well as committee endeavours. It will not be possible here to secure numerical results in terms of learner achievement. Tests are minimized by existentialists when obtaining data pertaining to achievement. Rather the pupil reveals progress, among other ways, through research in reading, writing prose and poetry, dramatic endeavours, pantomiming, art work, story telling, and making of objects and items, among others. Again, the feeling dimension is very salient when pupils reveal in processes and products that which has been learned. People posses feelings, thought, and action when participating in daily activities. Subject matter to be learned should reflect the human dilemma with its anxiety, stresses, and dread. Many materials of instruction will be necessary when existentialism as a philosophy of education is implemented. Audio visual aids, reading materials, art items, and other materials of instruction need to be there. Many inputs are needed so that pupils may reveal progress in variety of ways such as in the quality of written work, dramatizations, reading endeavours with related discussions, and art products, among others that stress creativity, not conformity behaviour.

Philosophy of Idealism

A teacher adhering to idealism stresses a subject centred curriculum. The academic areas receive much emphasis here. The abstract learning opportunities of listening well, speaking clearly, reading effectively with comprehension, and writing fluently should receive priority in a subject centred curriculum stressing vital academic content. Subject matter learned needs to be challenging, accurate, and relevant. Materials of instruction should include reading for a variety of intellectual purposes, technology to stress pupils interacting with and listening to vital subject matter, computers and word processors for writing activities, and models to improve speaking effectiveness. Inputs are important here in that costs are involved in having pupils attain vital objectives of instruction. Outputs could bring in testing and measuring; however, there are many other useful procedures to ascertain what pupils have learned. These include using portfolios, discussing academic subject matter, listening to and analyzing the contents pertaining to a significant debate involving the academics, writing for a variety of purposes, and reading significant content involving vital concepts, facts, and generalizations.

Idealists tend to emphasize intellectual development of pupils as being of utmost importance. Thus higher cognitive objectives are of primary significance, not affective nor psychomotor objectives. Affective (attitudinal) goals become salient if cognitive objectives are being achieved better than would otherwise be the case. The same can be said of psychomotor ends. Attaining relevant psychomotor ends are important to the degree that they assist learners in attaining cognitive or intellectual goals. Mental development is extremely significant in its development according to idealism as a philosophy of education.

Many inputs are needed when pupils are taught in a manner emphasizing intellectual growth. There should then be an adequate number of trade/library books as well as audiovisual aids being comprehensive in number so that pupils may be guided in developing appropriate thinking skills. Basal textbooks need to be challenging and on diverse reading levels. Concrete materials used in teaching must reflect higher levels of intellectual achievement. Inputs then are very important so that pupils do well taught by a teacher or teaching team stresses idealism as philosophy of education.

In Closing

Each philosophical school of thought in education has implications for helping to determine the amount of money involved in ascertaining how much of costs there will be in terms of inputs. Realism, focusing upon ends in teaching, requires the least in input when stressing financial input needed to buy school supplies. However, that could be debatable. For a teacher to assist pupils to attain behaviourally stated objectives, he/she must select appropriate learning opportunities so that learners attain optimally. Realists do view ends of instruction much more so than the means or learning opportunities to achieve objectives.

Experimentalists, existentialists, and idealists as philosophies of teaching and learning do require considerable emphasis being placed upon inputs. Thus to supply teachers here with materials of instruction requires considerable money. The experimentalist teacher bases instruction upon experiences provided in the curriculum. Experiences need to be rich and abundant so that the pupil with teacher guidance may identify and solve problems. Learning stations for an existentialist teacher also require a variety of concrete, semiconcrete, and abstract learning opportunities. Pupils may then select, from among alternatives, that which has interest, purpose, and value in learning. The idealist teacher focuses upon abstract materials of instruction to emphasize a subject centred curriculum. However, the concrete and the semiconcrete materials may be needed so that pupils achieve well in the symbolic domains.

The writers recommend the following:

1. using materials of instruction which harmonize with the individual styles of learners in achieving more optimally;
2. applying the best of each of the four philosophical approaches in learning. Thus quality precise objectives will be stressed in teaching. Problems solving will receive much stress since life itself consists of identification and solutions to problems. Decision making strategies also will receive much attentions since individuals need to select from among alternatives in life and living. Abstract thinking is salient since ultimately learning stresses thinking symbolically. Since the concrete and semiconcrete world of learning may not be available at a given time and place, thinking in the abstract truly is vital.

11

What Kind of Schools Do We Want? —A Public Debate

There is much debate and discussion as to the kind of education that is wanted for pupils in the public schools. People differ from each other in terms of objectives, learning opportunities, and evaluation procedures that should be emphasized in the school curriculum. The following scenario will indicate the nature of the difficulties in agreeing upon what makes for a good school. Different professors in a creative presentation will indicate their preferences in providing for quality in education.

Setting of the Debate

The professors in the debate are seated in front of the auditorium in a High School. After the introductions have been made for each presenter. Professor A is given the time explain what an ideal curriculum is.

We need to establish high standards for all pupils to attain in science. No learner should be left out of achieving these high standards. Any pupil left out will not obtain the sophisticated krowledge that is needed to be successful in society. We must have mixed achievement levels in all classrooms, not the evils of tracking. Once pupils are placed in a track, they always stay in that same track. Those who learn at a slower rate are then placed in and stay in the same track throughout their school years. In a democracy, we cannot afford to segregate pupils along class lines. In a competitive world, we cannot afford to have a pupil achieve at a lower level than what the high standards that have been developed for achievement indicate. Teachers need to have high expectations in science for all pupils so they can attain these high demanding standards. Perhaps, it will be necessary to have tutoring for a few pupils who are struggling to achieve the identified standards. However, in general, if pupils do not achieve these demanding goals and standards, then teachers have not taught them. America 2000 stresses world class standards. We in the United States are in competition with Japan, Germany, and other nations to capture our fair share of the world's economic markets. So let us get busy in establishing high standards for pupils to achieve in science in public school classrooms. Let us have the same high standards for each and every pupil. With high expectations for each learner, we can have all learners attain demanding, complex objectives. If expectations differ from one set of pupils to the other, some will not be taught the sophisticated knowledge necessary for a democracy. This means that teachers should focus only or largely upon the academics, not vocational courses. We must not segregate pupils into the academic versus the vocational track. If we do, democracy and individual pupil achievement in the academics go by the wayside.

Professor B. I can agree with much of what Professor A has just said. We do want to work toward equity and equality among pupils. Thus a focus upon the academics and heterogeneous grouping are musts. In a democracy, we must avoid segregating learners into groups where labels are used to identify each group. We do need to go one step further and that is to have cooperative learning in science. In cooperative learning, selected pupils who take a little longer to learn vital concepts and generalizations may be assisted in cooperative learning by those who achieve the same learning rather rapidly.

Research has shown that pupils learn better in cooperative learning settings as compared to other plans of grouping pupils for instruction. Slower achievers may be helped by those who attain concepts and generalizations readily. The teacher then becomes a guide and facilitator. Pupils enjoy working in groups and collegiality is important in any endeavour be it in school or in society. We need to emphasize collaboration now in the classroom if we went future workers to be able to work well with others in the work place. Why do teachers minimize cooperative learning endeavours in science (Ediger, 1994)? Research indicates that pupils achieve more when heterogeneous grouping is used in group endeavours, rather than having pupil work on individual projects and activities. We cannot afford in a democracy to segregate pupils by ability nor to work on boring knowledge.

Professor C. I think professors A and B have missed the point in the debate about what makes for a quality education for all. The free enterprise system has always aided in making for a good society. The United States has been a leader in the free enterprise system for two centuries. Let us use the excellent model of the free enterprise system to make for excellence in our schools. Therefore, we need to have parents choose which school their offspring is to attend. Furthermore, parents should also choose the teacher they want for their child. Suburban schools tend to be quite good as compared to the inner city and rural schools. Is it any wonder that pupils do not achieve as well in inner city and rural schools, as compared to pupils in suburban schools? Lets have parents select the school and teacher for their children and you will see that all pupils will achieve more optimally. If pupils are locked into the poorer schools such as those in the inner city and rural areas, is it any wonder that they do not do well in goal attainment? The free enterprise system will make it so that good teachers will have a great demand for their services whereas poor teachers will be weeded out of the teaching profession. Parental choice of schools and teachers for their offspring is the heart of a democracy. The market place has always served the United States well with competition among goods and services offered to consumers. Why do we fail our children by dictating where they are to attend school? It is no wonder that public schools are criticized for poor quality education. We need to promote competition among schools and among teachers for their services. Bad schools and teachers will then come to an end. Democracy is at a crossroads unless we permit parents to choose and select the kind of science education desired for their children.

Professor D. My friend here, professor C believes that parents should choose which school and teacher their children should have. Bad schools and teachers will then be weeded out. That is preposterous! How can parents know where the good educational programmes are? Will they be influenced by quality education or how good a basketball team or influential cheer leading team the schools have? There are an endless number of questions I would like to raise about the free enterprise system of school/teacher selection by parents; most of all who pays for transportation costs to and from school. Remember, there are many, many people living on the poverty level who also want the best education for their offspring. I would therefore recommend that every school district do needs survey to determine which objectives pupils are to attain. An effective survey of parents, teachers, administrators, and pupils themselves, can provide excellent data on which objectives learners are to achieve in school. Teachers and administrators can develop the questionnaire and field test it prior to mailing to respondents. An open space can be located in the questionnaire for respondents to write other objectives than those listed. One can weigh the questionnaire items so that parental input may have more effect than that of other respondents. From questionnaire results, one can notice objectives that are truly dear to the hearts and minds of school personnel and parents. I believe that there is dissatisfaction in public schools due to emphasizing the trivia and the unimportant in the curriculum. We will find out what is relevant in the science curriculum by obtaining responses from diverse segments in society. Then people in the community have a much better chance of being satisfied with the schools as compared to what is now the case. Why not improve all public schools rather than weeding out schools in inner city and rural areas because pupils are not achieving as well as in the suburban schools? A true democracy will attempt to provide all pupils with the very best science education possible in a readily accessible area.

Professor E. I think so far that we have all barked up the wrong tree in stating the cause and desire for improved education for all. We cannot improve our public schools if there is so much poverty in society. With a twenty per cent poverty rate of pupils attending our public schools, is it any wonder that pupils do not achieve well? How many of us on this panel would do well if we were hungry and/or lived on the streets, like street people? We panel members have Ph.D. or Ed.d. degrees and live in an ivory tower. We need to get out into the real world and notice people who are hungry, live in unsanitary conditions, and have inappropriate clothes. It is easy to sit here and theorize on what makes for good schools when we have ample food and then some, new expensive suits and dresses, new cars, and a fancy hotel/motel room to stay in for this debate. I have often wondered what is meant by the concept of democracy. The free enterprise system spreads people out from the extremely rich to the extreme poverty level. There are many 'war zones' in the US where fire arms, drugs, murders, rapes, teen age pregnancies, among other items abound. The late A.H. Maslow emphasized that meeting physiological and safety needs are the first two needs which must be met of individuals before other needs can be tackled such as learning subject matter. We need economic democracy. Merely having the right to vote for candidates desiring office does not make for a democracy. We need to lobby governmental officials to provide jobs which pay adequately for all workers. When jobs are not available such as in a recession or depression, welfare payments and other social programmes must be in the offing. Even in times of prosperity, unemployment benefits must be available to those in need. The business world has not kept its side of the bargain in reducing welfare recipients due to the lack of work opportunities. Let us in our schools work more and more in the direction of fulfilling physiological and safety needs of pupils. Once these needs are taken care of, pupils will achieve more of the goals of science in the school curriculum.

Professor F. I believe we must look at society realistically and notice all the changes that are occurring therein. Change is all around us. When I started teaching in the university in 1962, typewriters existed in all typing classes and offices on the campus. Where is the typewriter now? It is nonexistent on campuses and places of business in society and has become a museum piece. I do not even see a typewriter in anybody's office today nor do I see one in the business world! That is just one of numerous examples of changes in society. Since change is so rapid in school and society, why not emphasize processes and skills that are truly vital for all pupils to learn in science? I am speaking here of problem solving, critical and creative thinking. All people have problems, be it as a pupil in school or as a worker in society. Individuals may have problems pertaining to learning subject matter, skills, and attitudes in science. All curriculum areas could stress a problem solving curriculum in which pupils with teacher assistance identify questions and problems in ongoing lessons and units of study. Learners may then secure necessary information in arriving at a tentative solution. Knowledge, skills, and attitudes are tentative, not absolutes. Critical and creative thinking are an inherent part of problem solving since information to solve the identified problem needs to be analyzed. Creative solutions to problems are necessary, The 'tried and the true' as solutions do not work in most problems. Change is always a key element in any situation. Life does not stand still, but newness, novelty, and openess are in evidence (Ediger, 1994). Therefore, let us as educators in all of our classes emphasize problem solving as a major objective in all curriculum areas. Academic subject matter learned by individuals may soon be forgotten or becomes obsolete. Knowledge changes in terms of what we know and how we perceive it. Democracy emphasizes that we have and develop individuals who can truly identify and solve problems. These problems in science are there as all of you panel members have indicated.

Chairman of the panel. I personally wish to thank each panel member for taking the time and putting forth the effort to make an excellent presentation here this evening. No doubt the audience has questions that they would wish to address to a certain panel member. Would you speak clearly into the microphone at your nearby station? Yes, go ahead at station one.

Audience member. I would like to address a question to Professor F. You have not stated your position on which relevant subject matter pupils are to achieve. Don't you think that there is vital subject matter that all pupils should achieve? Later on in life, pupils should be able to use the knowledge and skills acquired in the science and school curriculum. I believe there are basics or essentials in science subject matters which all pupils need to attain. Former President Ronald Reagan and former Secretary of Education William Bennett always stated that teachers should teach the basics only.

Professor F. There is no subject matter that is of importance unless it is used as a means to an end and that end being problem solving. I see no value in learning subject matter unless it has use and is utilitarian. Too frequently, pupils are drilled on and memorize subject matter taught for no apparent reason. What happens then? Pupils forget what has been committed at the time to rote memory. What is useful and applicable will be remembered longer in science than that which has no value, except it will appear on a test (Ediger and Rao, 1996).

Audience member #2. My question is directed to Professor B. I have a gifted daughter who needs a challenging curriculum based on her level of achievement and pace as well as her ability level. She definitely is not motivated in a regular classroom. Professor B, you did not mention any specific curriculum for the gifted except to help slow learners in the classroom catch up with other pupils in the classroom in cooperative learning. Why did you omit the gifted in your presentation? I subscribe to the Gifted Child Quarterly and in the Spring 1992 issue in an article entitled 'Grouping Cifted Students', the author talks about lower achievement and poorer attitudes on the part of gifted pupils if they are in heterogeneously grouped classrooms.

Professor B. Having an elite curriculum for the gifted is undemocratic. The gifted can generally learn and achieve on their own with minimal teacher assistance. They do not need much teacher assistance. Let us rather concentrate on the slower achievers and bring all pupil up to the same/similar level of achievement. Democratic theory emphasizes we are all equal before the law. Thomas Jefferson, author of the Declaration of Independence, stated that all men are created equal. Let us look at an implement the democratic concept of equity for all. Gifted pupils truly learn much in science when they assist and teach the slower achievers.

Audience member #3. I wish to address my question to Professor A. How will all pupils in a class achieve the same demanding standards? There are slow, average, and fast achievers in any classroom, especially with heterogeneously grouped pupils.

Professor A. Too frequently teachers have low expectations for selected pupils such as the 'slow' learner. Perhaps, there is no such a being. We teachers and educators place pupils into categories and give them labels. These labels affect how pupils learn and behave. Is it not better to teach all pupils instead of categorizing them? Pupils will be hindered if they did not receive sophisticated knowledge in science which the better achiever received. Do you want your son/daughter to receive inferior teachers, instruction, and simpler knowledge? I am sure you will answer in the negative. High expectations from learners and good teaching is the answer to your question. For a democratic society, pupils need to experience a curriculum of equity.

Audience member #4. I wish to address my question to Professor C. Are you aware of hunger and poverty in the US? How can anyone learn who is living in an atmosphere of needing food, clothing, and shelter? Toward the other end of this extreme are the very wealthy persons living in the US. I have taken guided tours of different wealthy areas of the US such as Atlanta, Georgia to notice the homes of billionaires. Some of these houses have the size of the White House in Washington, DC. These and others are truly luxurious beyond description. These are just examples of the homes of the many billionaires and multi-millionaires in the US. Then I have driven through slum areas with its broken windows, paper strewn about here and there, as well as empty burned out buildings, block after block. TV newscasts have shown war zone areas in the US where parents worry on a daily basis if their offspring will survive in safety from day to day. These parents also worry about the young joining gangs. A competitive society has just not helped many Americans. I do not think your plan of parental selection of schools and teachers has been thought through carefully. Can parents truly choose the best education for their child? Will the better schools be bombarded with parents who want their children enrolled therein? Isn't the reason for suburbia having better pupil achievement based on wealth within the district? How will all pupils be transported to the schools of choice and who pays for the transportation costs? Should we not rather try to improve all schools rather than have the mass confusion of parental choice, due to poverty in many of the poor achieving districts?

Professor C. Throwing money at schools does not solve problems. People are not motivated to change and improve unless there is competition. I achieved well in the public school because of being highly motivated to be at the top of the class in performance. I grew up in poverty on a farm. The depression years had taken its toll of my parents. Early in life, I saw the need to achieve and do well in school. I spoke the high German and the Low German Languages only when entering the public school years. I learned to speak English on the first grade level. After the first semester ended, the teacher asked me to pronounce words to those having trouble identifying words when reading silently. You raise yourselves up by your own bootstraps. My mother had a devastating stroke when I was in the fifth grade which almost immediately made it so that my older brother, a junior in high school, and I did the farm chores. My father took care of my invalid mother who became like a vegetable. My older sister took over most of the housework when she was an eighth grader. There was no talk about divorce or placing mother in a nursing home. I made it very successfully through the ED.D. degree. Why can we not apply the tenets of free enterprise and competition to the availability of good schools for pupils? Let the laws of supply and demand apply to those schools that will survive and endure as compared to those that just school not be. It is as simple as that!

Audience member #5. I would like to have my question addressed to Professor E. You did not address which subject matter goals, especially in science, pupils should attain (Ediger, 1996). You largely focused on meeting basic needs of pupils such as food, clothing, and shelter, among others. What should pupils learn in terms of science, mathematics, social studies, and reading/literature?

Professor E. Once the basic needs of survival for pupils are met, then pupils have an inward desire to learn. Intrinsic, not extrinsic motivation, of learners is needed. The present economic system leaves much to be desired. In school, the teacher and pupil need to plan together what the latter is to learn in science. But it is if pupils individually may select, from among alternatives, what he/she is to learn. Learning to make choices and decisions is the heart of life and living. In a democracy, pupils individually need to choose what they wish to learn. Pupils should not compete against each other, but rather work on task that are fulfilling and enjoyable. Pupils start to learn when they can pursue personal interests and purposes in the curriculum. Why should they study what is dictated to them from state mandated objectives as well as from others in the educational arena? Pupils learn when interest and purpose propels their motivation for learning.

Audience member # 6. My question is addressed to Professor D. So many surveys have been made of what pupils are to learn and do as a result of instruction... An enormous number of studies and recommendations are being made on what pupils are to learn in terms of subject matter and skills. I am a science teacher and the National Science Teacher Association came out with an excellent set of objectives for pupils to attain. Why do Professors continually emphasize surveys and studies to be made to determine what pupils are to learn? Don't you believe we have enough objectives available based on prestigious study groups to last us a long time without spinning more wheels nor reinventing the wheel?

Professor D. National study groups have done an excellent job in assisting to determine what pupils are to learn. The NSTA study that you referred to was one of the first national organisations to come out with a set of goals for learner attainment. They spent much time and money in developing these outstanding standards. The National Council for the Social Studies, The National Council Teachers of Mathematics, The National Council for Geographic Education, among others, have indeed invested much in securing for teacher and administrator use those objectives that pupils are to attain as a result of teaching. We all need to read, study, and ponder over these objectives. These objectives may be implemented as desired into the school curriculum. I also believe that locally we need to determine what parents in particular want for their children in terms of an education of excellence. Only by a survey of educators and the lay public can we ascertain what it is that people want in science in order to emphasize a quality curriculum. In a rapidly changing society, we need to be knowledgeable of objectives that pertain to the subject matter areas which we teach. What is a better way to emphasize democracy than when there is input from all involved people in a given school or school distract. Democracy is at the heart of my procedure in obtaining vital goals for pupils attainment.

Chairperson. I see so many hands that would like to ask additional questions of these panel members. However, our time is up. Thank you for coming!

REFERENCES

American Educational Research Association (1992). *Handbook of Research on Curriculum*. New York: Macmillan Company.

Delta Kappa Gamma Bulletin (1994). The Teaching Crisis, 60, 4.

Ediger, Marlow, and D. Bhaskara Rao, (1996). *Science Curriculum*. New Delhi, India: Discovery Publishing House, Chapter Eight.

Ediger, Marlow (1994). Gifted Students in Mathematics. *Journal of Instructional Psychology*, 29, 120-124.

Ediger, Marlow (1994). Computer in Science. *School Science*, 1-4, Published in India by the National Council for Educational Research and Training (NCERT).

Ediger, Marlow (1988). *The Elementary Curriculum*. Kirksville, Missouri: Simpson Publishing Company. Chapter Seven—Issues in the Curriculum, 59-69.

Ediger, Marlow (1996). Reading in Science. *School Science*, 50-56.

Ediger, Marlow (1994). Project Methods in Middle School Science. *New Mexico Middle School Journal*. 24-26.

Geography Education Standards Project (1994). *Geography for Life; What Every Young American Should Know and be able to do in Geography*. Washington, DC: Geography Education Standards Project.

International Reading Association/National Council Teachers of English Joint Task Force on Assessment (1994). *Standards for the Assessment of Reading and Writing*. Nework, Del./Urbana, III,: IRA/NCTE.

National Council for the Social Studies (1994). *Curriculum Standards for Social Studies*: Expectations of Excellence. Washington, DC: NCSS.

National Council Social Studies Task Force on Scope and Sequence (1984). *In search of a scope and sequence for social studies*. Social Education 48, 249-262.

National Council Teachers of Mathematics (1989). *Curriculum and Evaluation Standards for School Mathematics*. Reston, Virginia: NCTM.

National Science Teachers Association (1997), *National Science Educational Standards*. Arlington, Virginia: NSTA.

National Society for the Study of Education (1994). *Teacher Research and Educational Reform*. Chicago, Illinois: NSSE.

Richardson, Michael D., and others (1993). *Schools Principals and Change*. New York: Garland Publishing, Inc.

12

Reading Comprehension in the Science Curriculum

Science teachers need to be teachers of reading since the fact of being able to read and comprehend is necessary in problem solving activities. There should be a variety of learning opportunities in ongoing lessons and units of study, and reading subject matter is one important facet of achieving. It certainly is true that some classrooms stress reading of content to the point that other kinds of experiences are almost nonexistent. Reading is one approach in learning in science.

What might the teacher do to assist pupils to comprehend science subject matter more thoroughly in reading? There is always the problem of new words that pupils cannot identify in reading science content. How should these situations be handled? We will offer several suggestions that my student teachers and cooperating teachers whom we supervised in the schools used.

1. A good reader pronounces words that are unknown to pupils as they read silently. As a first grader during the 1934-35 school year, and later elementary schools years also, one of us was asked by the classroom teacher to pronounce unknown words to pupils when they raised their hands during silent

reading. This approach can be overdone if the same pupil is asked sequentially to pronounce unknown words to others. Pupils individually would also like to pursue their own reading interests. Sometimes, a pupil pronounces an unknown word too quickly to a learner, not permitting adequate time for the latter to ascertain what the unknown words is. If a pupil does not know what the unknown is, he/she should have enough time to determine what the correct word is. The opposite situation occurs also whereby a pupil has to wait too long to obtain help with identification of unknown words when reading science content.

2. The teachers should write new words on the chalkboard in neat manuscript letters prior to pupils reading a selection in science. He/she needs to go over each printed word several times pupils in class. The teacher needs to be certain that pupils are looking at each word as it is being pronounced by the teacher or individual pupils. Using this approach assists pupils to see the new words on the chalkboard in print before seeing them while reading. Hopefully learners will recognize each word as it is being read in science.

The printed words may be written individually or within a sentence on the chalkboard. We prefer the latter approach since it is more contextual. Pupils may learn to use context clues more thoroughly when seeing new words printed within sentences. Learners need to attach meaning to these new words. Context clues many times provide the needed information for pupils to understand needed meanings. Sometimes, a word needs to be defined so that pupils know intended meanings and can read content more proficiently.

3. Cassette recordings may be made of science content pupils are to read, be it from the basal or from a library book. The teacher need not always make these recordings, if his/her schedule is very busy. We have observed good readers make excellent cassette recordings of science subject matter. The same content may be listened to by a reader as he/she reads

sequential ideas from a book. If the reader does not identify selected words in context, the recorded voice will provide the necessary information. This approach can be used very successfully when pupils read in science. Carlo (1996) wrote:

For many young children and poor readers, there's a substantial time lag between when they see and hear a word. That lag produces slow, laborious reading that makes comprehension all but impossible. It's terribly difficult for students to recall what a passage is about when they have to spend so much time figuring out each new word.

A recorded book can, in effect, do what the child is not yet able to do naturally. It verbalizes the printed words with the correct pace, phrasing, and expression. As a result students make fewer reading errors, and the possibility of forming incorrect reading patterns is diminished.

Best of all, it's not necessary to recall dull, simple reading materials to develop a student's sight vocabulary.

4. Instead of reading from the basal text, pupils may read subject matter from library books related to the ongoing lesson or unit of study. There needs to be an adequate number of library books so that a learner may choose a book that is on his/her reading level. We observed several lessons in schools where this procedure worked very successfully. Pupils would then share with the entire class that which had been read. Ediger (1996) wrote:

One approach in emphasizing sequence is to have students choose the order of experience within a flexible environment. Thus, for example, in individualized reading, a learner selects which library books to read sequentially. After reading a book, the pupil has a conference with the teacher to appraise progress. After the completion of the conference with the teacher, the learner is ready to select the next library book to read. The teacher intervenes in library book selection if the student is unable to choose and complete reading a book.

In situations involving individualized reading in science, the pupil orders his/her own experiences. Sequence, it is felt, resides within the involved learner. Others, the teacher included, cannot select the order of goals for a learner to attain. The student in individualized reading must do the processing of content. A teacher determined science reading curriculum does not work, according to advocates of individualized reading Humanism, as a psychology of learning, strongly advocates concepts such as the following:

1. student-teacher planning of the science curriculum;
2. learners choosing from diverse objectives which to achieve and which to omit;
3. learning centres from which pupils may select their learning opportunities;
4. students being involved in determining objectives within a contract systems. In contract from, the pupil with teacher guidance plans which experiences to complete along with the date of completion. Both pupil and teacher sign the contractual agreement in science;
5. a good reader might read the selection for the day from the basal science text orally to slower learners in reading. The latter may follow along in their own textbooks as the words are read orally. These participants may be seated close together in an atmosphere of respect so that optimal listening is involved. The good reader should explain difficult concepts to pupils as they are being met in print. After hearing the science content read orally, we have noticed slow readers who desire to read the entire selection to themselves;
6. peer teaching can be quite effective in reading science content. With peer teaching, two or three pupils read the contents orally from the basal text; each follows along in his/her book as the other reads. If a slow reader does not wish to read orally, the other two pupils may do the oral reading. These learners may also discuss salient ideas from the science content read. The goal in all of these reading endeavours is to assist pupils to

comprehend and understand science content, not to ridicule or minimize. Respect for others is always salient in each science lesson and unit of study;

7. we have observed where no basal texts are used in science and pupils read content from library books directly related to the unit being taught in the science curriculum. Pupils then have done an outstanding job of telling what was read as it relates to the ongoing discussion in thematic unit teaching. Pupils individually tend to select library books that are on their reading level to comprehend well. We believe many pupils feel more at ease reading from library books as compared to the basal. Canney and Neuenfeldt (1993) wrote:

Most elementary teachers still use a basal for reading instruction. However, it appears that teachers combine children's book and basals, which is a change from previous reports. Teachers perceive themselves to be in line with school district policy to support their preference for a basal/tradebooks combination. Most teachers also say that they have access to an adequate supply of tradebooks and 85 per cent believe that children should read independently for 15 to 30 minutes daily. Finally, regardless of teaching experience, formal training in reading, or grade level taught, most teachers prefer a combination of basal and tradebooks in their reading programmes.

One of the authors has also successfully observed whereby two volunteers from the community assisted selected learners who had difficulty identifying words in reading from the science textbooks. The volunteers listed carefully to pupils read orally in a designated area. They helped pupils with recognizing unknown words and pronouncing selected words to these as learners was needed. Seemingly, these same pupils were then ready to read the same science selection on their own. They were also able to enter the discussions effectively in the classroom pertaining to what had been read.

9. there are teachers who have simplified content contained in the text. By using less complex words

and shorter sentences, selected pupils might now read and understand the revised subject matter. Generally, teachers have confided in me that the approach is good but the work involved in rewriting takes up an excessive amount of time;

10. sometimes, slow readers have read well from the basal after having listened to the class discussion covering the related subject matter. By listening carefully to the discussion, slow readers may be able to read the same content from the basal science textbook due to possessing readiness information for reading. We are not entirely in agreement with this procedure; however, the teacher needs to assist pupils with a variety of procedures in word recognition and comprehension so that each pupil may attain more optimally in the science curriculum. McNinch and Gruber (1996) wrote:

What children, ultimately learn about literacy is heavily influenced by the expectations, skills and concerns that parents, teachers, and principals share. All players in literacy development should possibly share common perceptions, especially in the basic philosophical and pedagogical beliefs, if children are to receive coordinated instruction. Do parents, teachers, and principals agree on the basic reading issue of whole language versus traditional skill development?...

Parents, teachers, and principals each perceived that the development of literacy in young children is developed broadly both through traditional practices and whole language, emerging literacy routines. This research groups find favour with traditional readiness activities...Also, they perceive that children learn literacy as an emerging activity through such activities as repetitive listening, shared story telling, invented spelling, and creative writing.

Emerging literacy is a mutual product of the home and school environment acting together with common interests. It does appear that the literacy providers, parents and teachers, are supporting each other in an electric approach to learning.

How Much Assistance Should be Given In Word Recognition Techniques?

There is no easy answer to this question. So often, it is felt and believed that the teacher of reading alone should assist pupils in word recognition and identification. A problem then results with pupils who need much guidance to identify unknown words in reading in the content fields, such as in science. Certainly, pupil achievement, in part, will be due to how well a learner reads and comprehends subject matter to solve problems. Thus, it behooves the teacher to assist pupils in reading science materials. The more that reading is stressed as a means of learning the more likely it will be that pupils need assistance in word recognition.

There are six word recognition skills that pupils need to develop skill in. The use of picture clues to unlock unknown words will be used more so on the early primary grade levels as compared to later times. Why? There are more pictures in a basal science text on the early primary grade levels as compared to later times. If a first grader, for example, does not know a word, he/she may look at a picture on the same page and the unknown word will usually become known. There are exceptions here so the primary grade pupil, as well as at later sequential stages of learning, will need to learn additional procedures, other than using picture clues, to unlock unknown words.

Phonics is taught more than any other technique to unlock unknown words. There are degrees of regularity in using phonics to recognize words. Thus there are many sound/symbol relationships that are consistent in the English language. The words-ban, can, dan, fan, man, nan, pan, ran, tan- follow a consistent spelling between each grapheme and phoneme. Sometimes, only a few letters in a word will have consistent spelling between symbol and sound, such as the following words-globe, scale, miles and agriculture. Selected words are spelled very irrationally, such as through, bough, cough, bought, and dough. Thus, there are words or word parts that need to be learned through the sight method, not phonics. Learning words through the sight method makes it so that the learner has no approach to use to unlock unknown words in science.

The use of context clues is a very valuable procedure to use to unlock an unknown word in science. Thus if a pupil does not know how to pronounce a word, he/she looks careful at the surrounding words and may be able to identify a word that fits in and makes sense. Sometimes, there are not enough clues in the surrounding words to assist in determining what the unknown word is, such as "I see a ... There are too many words that make sense contextually. But if the reader uses phonics also, perhaps the unknown can be identified, such as "I see a I..." Here, the 'I' letter is very consistent in sound and the pupil may now be able to determine what fits in.

The use of syllabication skills may prove very helpful to the reader to unlock unknown words in science. A word that appears to be new and unknown, may not be so if the pupil divides the 'unknown' into syllabus, for example, the word 'unimportant' looks long until the pupil notices the prefix 'un'. If the pupil knows the prefix 'un' means 'not', then it should be very possible to identify and attach meaning to an unknown word. Many prefixes and suffixes appear again and again in reading and the pupil soon becomes skillful in dividing a science word into syllables to identify and pronounce it correctly.

We recommend that teachers of science be teachers of reading and assist pupils to learn approaches in word recognition which make for independent readers. Science lessons and units do emphasize reading as a means of acquiring information; therefore, pupils need to comprehend subject matter through reading.

Diverse Purpose in Reading

There are many purposes for reading in science and not one purpose or reason only. Comprehension of science content is an overall goal. Certainly, pupils should read for meaning and not for the sake of going through the motions only. The concept of 'comprehension' needs to be broken down to more specific aims in the reading of science content. We believe that reading to solve problems in science should be the major goal. Most science educators put high priority in having pupils read to solve problems. Certainly, life in society demands that we identify and solve vital problem areas. There is much confusion as to what can be termed as a problem. Should these come from pupils only with teacher assistance? Might teachers select problems which pupils accept once readiness for learning has been developed? We have observed in classrooms where pupils do accept problems identified by teachers if there are stimulating ways of doing this. With stimulating audiovisual aids presented meaningfully to capture learner interest, pupils might well accept teacher identified problems in science for solving.

In addition to reading to solve science problems, pupils should read critically. Here pupils analyze subject matter read. When analyzing, learners separate component parts so that each facet may be assessed thoroughly or at the developmental level of the learner. We have observed pupils debate the accuracy of selected statements after analyzing. Reference books and other sources are looked at to check accuracy. There are many slogans that abound in society and these may be found in content being viewed carefully by pupils. Are slogans, for example, like the following true?

1. That government is best which governs least. Is there a chance that so little government makes for anarchy?
2. It's not guns that kill, but people kill.
3. Let's get government off our backs and out of our pockets.
4. Let's not throw money at problems.
5. Long prison sentences deter crime.

Each slogan should be evaluated in terms of being based on evidence or are they myths? Sometimes, the bandwagon approach is in evidence in society in that everyone joins the majority in whatever is being stressed. For example, in the early 1970s, performance contracting came in big into American education. Thus the business world entered the educational arena by contracting for providing educational services to public schools. They promised larger gains in pupil achievement that what traditional approaches could produce. For every pupil that achieved, according to what was in the business contract, the company would receive that amount as specified in the agreement. There were many schools wanting to join in on performance contracting since 'pupils' would achieve at a higher level.' This plan soon fizzled out in that pupils did poorer as compared to using traditional approaches in teaching. Second, many teachers taught directly to the test in performance contracting which other schools could not do. Teaching directly to the test items should make for higher achievement if test results are used to determine pupil progress. Performance contracting has reappeared but under much less publicity and fanfare, such as in Educational Alternatives, based in Minneapolis, Minnesota. The band wagon approach needs to be analyzed in critical thinking situations. "The everybody is doing it" philosophy can be very harmful to individuals and groups in society, as well as in the science curriculum.

Pertaining to critical reading, Harris and Sipay (1985) wrote:

> An important kind of critical reading involves comparison of two or more sources of information. Children are usually amazed when they first find two authorities contradicting each other. An experience like that can serve as a preliminary to discussion of such questions as the reputation and prestige of each author, his impartiality, or bias, the comparative recency of the two sources, and so on. Reading experiences of this sort develop naturally when children do wide reading to find data on a problem. The teacher should be alert and should make use of such occasions as stepping stones toward a more mature attitude on the credibility of reading matter. In the study of current events, comparison of the treatment of an event by two newspapers or magazines of opposing points of view can form an effective point of departure.

A second kind of critical reading involves considering new ideas or information in the light of one's previous knowledge and beliefs. The thoughtful reader asks... It is reasonable. Is it possible? He does not, of course, automatically reject the unfamiliar idea or challenging conclusion... But...becomes doubly alert when he finds disagreements with what he has previously accepted as true.

Creative thinking is another relevant goal for pupils to achieve in reading science content. Learners need to be able to brainstorm and come up with unique, novel ideas in ongoing lessons and units of study. In the area of reading science content, pupils, for example, might have heard the following:

1. the planet Saturn has a solid core or ring around itself;
2. there is no relationship between dinosaurs and birds on the evolutionary scale;
3. amphibians are not becoming fewer in number on the planet earth;
4. all dinosaurs were cold blooded animals.

The teacher needs to stimulate pupils to raise innovative questions as well as come up with unique responses to statements made by others or read from older reference sources. Thus pupils may come up with updated information pertaining to the above four statements. There are numerous ways that pupils can come up with creative answers to problem areas:

1. Have a committee read from a variety of recent reference sources and give a report to the class on ringlets that encircle the planet Saturn. Illustrations may be shown as the oral report is given. A model solar system might also assist pupils to understand content in the report.
2. Assist a committee to discuss and summarize contents on recent discoveries in Patagonia, Argentina pertaining to a possible linkage between dinosaurs

and birds in prehistoric times. A map should be used/drawn showing the region of these findings.

In addition to giving science reports, pupils may also show what has been learned through

1. the making of *dioramas*, models, movie sets, and flannel boards with cutouts;
2. dramatic activities including formal, creative, pantomime, and role playing;
3. outlining, summarizing, concluding, and paraphrasing;
4. developing parts for and presenting a reader's theatre presentation;
5. doing a collage, a bulletin board display, and an outside the classroom series of displays, placed on corridor walls;
6. engaging in discussions, debates, committee work, individual study plans, use of learning centres for enrichment, reading library books, and pupil/teacher planning of learning opportunities;
7. performing science experiments and demonstrations. This is the heart of the science curriculum.

In addition to problem solving, as well as creative and critical thinking in reading science content, pupils should also practice reading for causes and effects such as in the causes for natural disasters. Events read should be evaluated in terms of causes for happenings. This is a precise aim of reading instruction in the science curriculum. Pupils, then should use methods of acquiring and appraising information in the same way as does the professional scientist.

An additional skill in reading science content is reading for factual information. Sometimes, it seems, according to many educators, that factual acquisition is not necessary. But, this should not be the case. Facts provide the building blocks for pupils to use in developing concepts and generalizations. A relationship of facts, perceived accurately by the learner, should make for quality generalizations. Within a concept, there also are many facts. Look at the following generalization that might well be important for pupils to achieve in a unit on Rocks and Minerals:

1. There are igneous, sedimentary and metamorphic rocks. There are four concepts here—igneous, sedimentary, metamorphic, and rocks.

Inside of each concept, there are numerous facts. Thus the concept—igneous—refers to molten materials such as lava or magma that comes from the interior of the planet earth.

Reading for facts then is important to develop concepts and generalizations. Should facts be read for their own sake? We do much reading of subject matter and find factual reading for its own sake can be quite interesting and enjoyable. For example, we have found very little practical use for knowing facts pertaining the thinking of Aristotle in ancient Athens whereby he believed the brain to be the place of cooling of the human blood. We have noticed that many others do not find Aristotle interesting to read pertaining to his beliefs on physiology and the natural environment. Thus my undergraduate students, in most cases, cannot recall these events and yet all admit having studied Aristotle's philosophy on the human body and nature. Maybe, this says to us that much of what is learned in science is personal and purposeful to the individual. Thus the science teacher needs to have an ample number of reading activities selected/or designed for the individual. Cooperative learning in reading is important, but so are individual endeavours. The teacher needs to stress group endeavours as well as individual projects and experiences in reading.

Also, adequate emphasis should be place on how to do something in reading. We have noticed and observed pupils making models by following directions. Thus model cars, planes, trucks, among others, are assembled through reading. Here, pupils tend to perceive much purpose or reasons for reading. Teachers need to locate materials for pupils which the latter finds interesting and purposeful. These ingredients assist pupils to become better readers. Exercises in workbooks, textbooks, and project construction contain directions which need to be followed accurately. Wrong responses from pupils can come about if directions are not followed accurately and thoroughly. Pupils need much practice in reading to follow directions. They should be able to state directions read into their very own words so that meaning and understanding are there.

Pupils should develop skill early in the public school years of becoming research oriented. We believe that scanning information is very important. When we worked on our doctoral dissertations as well as on many other projects, we scanned the table of contents and articles in educational journals and textbooks to see of the content was relevant. The skill of scanning can be learned by pupils at a young age. Many of our pupils will be going on to higher education where this skill becomes important in locating information for term projects and papers developed. In the workplace, workers may also need to scan pages to see where relevant information is located, such as an automobile mechanic scanning pages in a manual to notice how to repair an air-conditioner in an older car.

Closely related to scanning is the reading skill of skimming content. Skimming also is a rather rapid type of reading since not every word is read when a person skims for a few ideas such as names, dates, and places. If a pupil reads to determine the birth and death of Louis Pasteur he/she will look for numerals in skimming an entire page or more. Or, if a learner is looking for Edward Jenner and his inoculation procedures for small pox the name of that person will have capital letters for each name. The capital letters set the name off from other subject matter on the page, except for the beginning of a sentence or the names of cities. Generally, there are very few items that start with capital letters on a page of content. Knowing this assists the individual in doing a better job of skimming, Pertaining to skimming, Ruben (1983) wrote:

Setting purposes for reading is a crucial factor in reading. Students need to learn that they read for different purposes.

If they are reading for pleasure, that may either read quickly or slowly based on the way they feel. If they are studying or reading information that is new to them, they will probably read very slowly. If, however, they are looking up a telephone number, a name, a date or looking over a paragraph for its topic, they will read much more rapidly. Reading rapidly to find or locate information is called *skimming*. All skimming involves fast reading: however, there are different kinds of skimming, skimming for a number, a date, or name can be done much more rapidly than skimming for the topic of a paragraph or to answer specific questions. (Some persons call the most rapid reading *scanning* and the less rapid reading *skimming*.) Teachers should help pupils recognize that they read rapidly to locate some specific information, but that once they have located what they want, they may read the surrounding information more slowly.

It is quite obvious that there are numerous purposes for reading in science. The purpose involved determines how rapidly one will read or how slowly. The amount of background information possessed as well as the complexity of the materials will also determine the rate at which something is read.

Teachers need to assess reading comprehension of pupils. Barr and Sadow (1985) wrote:

> An assessment of reading comprehension serves a twofold purpose. It enables the teacher to make an informed decision regarding the level of materials that would be appropriate for instruction, and it alerts the teacher to a student's scientific instructional needs. Such an assessment is generally undertaken when there is some question concerning a student's present placement in instructional materials or the type of instructional emphasis that would enable the student to make better progress. For the most part these questions arise when a student is not performing well during daily lessons. But they should arise also when a student is performing extremely well. For instructional materials should be neither so difficult that

the student can have little success with them nor so easy as to require little thought or attentional effort. Thus the student who is always able to answer the teacher's questions may need more challenging materials, while the student who can seldom answer questions correctly may need less demanding ones. Teachers must make every effort to see the instructional materials are optimal from this point of view.

How Should A Reading Assignment Be Introduced?

The science teacher should have several strategies available to guide pupils in reading a new selection. We would recommend first that the teacher try to ascertain which words in the lesson to be read, pupils may have difficulty with. Certainty is not involved here. The teacher, however, should know his/her pupils well enough to do a good job of hypothesizing which words pupils may have trouble identifying unless there is assistance prior to reading. We recommend that these words be printed on the chalkboard so that all can see them clearly written in sentences. Have pupils trade off reading an entire sentence with the new word therein. It is best if pupils get as much practice as possible in pronouncing what are perceived, by the teacher, to be new words. Go over the new words within sentences as often as is necessary so that pupils may master these words and identify them when reading science content silently. We would make certain that there is meaning and understanding of these new words as a part of learning to identify each word. Then too, we believe learners need to identify one or more reasons for reading in science. These reasons may be stated in question form and printed on the chalkboard. Thus pupils have a better idea as to what to read for and that being to obtain answers to questions.

After pupils have had a chance to read the selection silently or orally, the teacher may lead a discussion of science content read which may answer each question. The discussion should be relaxed and not hurried. Pupils need to have opportunities to think of possible answers to science questions. Questions raised by pupils other than what was read from the text may also be discussed.

I believe there should be enrichment activities for pupils following the discussion of the story read from the basal. The following are possibilities:

1. learners individually may read library books on the same topic or by the same author. The teacher needs to introduce selected library books to pupils to whet appetites for reading;
2. performing science experiments, dramatizing, pantomiming, model making, and constructing items that relate directly to content read can be good ways to make use of knowledge acquired;
3. rewriting the contents from the library book involving science fiction;
4. explaining the content orally or through reader's theatre might well be challenging for a few pupils;
5. writing test items in science to cover the contents in the reading selection can be interesting for selected learners. The test items may be exchanged among pupils in order to take the best. Pupils should receive feedback on the quality of their writing of each test item.

Selecting Science Textbooks

Teachers are generally involved in a committee to choose basal science textbook series for the oncoming school year. Certainly, each team member needs to have quality standards in mind when making textbook decisions. We have had numerous science teachers say to us that they believe the following criteria assisting in making the best choice possible:

1. The text needs to bring in a reasonable number of new concepts on each page or chapter. If too many new words are mentioned per page, the reading task could be overwhelmingly difficult. Should there be too

few new words per page, the book may lack challenge for pupils.

2. Pupils should have a chance to read from each series being considered for adoption to assist in determining which text would best meet the needs of learners.

3. The textbook being considered needs to be written in a style and manner which optimalize comprehension of contents.

4. There needs to be a helpful related manual for teacher use in choosing objectives, learning activities, and appraisal procedures. Generally, there are marginal notes which may assist teachers in the task of teaching science.

5. An ample number of illustrations and diagrams should be in evidence in each chapter to guide pupils to understand content more optimally.

6. The size of the type should be appropriate for the pupils who will be reading from the text.

7. There should be an adequate number of headings and subheadings in each selection or reading to orientate the learner to what the ensuing content will be about.

8. An adequate number of study aids for pupils should be in the textbook. Experimentalism should be at the heart of teaching science.

9. The textbook should contain an adequate number of summaries and previews for pupils.

10. There should be a table of contents, index, and glossary for pupil use. An index and glossary may not be in a text for young learners.

Participants on the committee to select the science text should invite comments from other teachers who will also be using the adopted textbook. Members of the selection team need to have available for all teachers and adequate number of science series so that decisions can be made on which text should be adopted. Comments made in the selection process should be courteous and clear. Respect for the thinking of others is important. Due consideration should be given each book. Slighting a series is not in the best interests of selecting a truly quality book in teaching science.

Personalized Reading in the Science Curriculum

There are times when pupils should select their very own library books to read that directly relate to the ongoing science unit. Generally, when pupils individually choose what is to be read, they select that which is interesting and on their very own reading level. The text may be too difficult for a few children to read even with quality methods of obtaining pupil readiness for reading a given selection. Thus an answer may be to have pupils individually choose a library book that has similar information as does the basal textbook.

After choosing a book, from among many others, the learner settles down to read the content. The teacher does not intervene unless a pupil cannot decide upon which book to read or gets bogged down on what is being pursued presently. If a pupil cannot decide upon which book to read, the teacher needs to provide assistance. If a pupil gets bogged down on what is read, the teacher needs to determine reasons for doing so. The following could be inherent reasons:

1. the book is too difficult for the pupil to read and understand;
2. the pupil needs to be encouraged to pursue what is difficult to read;
3. a peer approach may be used whereby two pupils change off reading the contents to each other and assist where there are problems;
4. the contents may be cassette recorded by a good reader and the involved pupil may listen to the contents, following along in his book, as the tape is being played. The learner then may be able to read the book on his/her own;
5. rewards may be given to honour those pupils who read a designated number of library books within an interval of time. Following the completion of the

reading of the library books, the learner may share the contents with others during discussion time in the ongoing science unit of study. The learner may also have a conference with the teacher to appraise comprehension and understanding of what had been read. The teacher may also check fluency of oral reading, word attack skills, and attitudes toward reading content in science. Ideally, the pupil should share during class discussions what was learned from reading library books. Each library book read relates directly to the ongoing lesson or unit of study in science being pursued.

Experience Charts in Science

Primary grade pupils, in particular, like to develop experience charts with teacher guidance. Although when pupils can do their very own writing, they should do so. As the name indicates, an experience chart relates directly to what pupils have experienced in science. For example, a first grade teacher may have the following objects on an interest centre to initiate a unit:

1. a model self-propelled combine and a tractor. Here, pupils may study simple machines, involved in physics, inherent in the combine and tractor;
2. model farm implements for the tractor to pull. A further study of simple machines involved in performing work may be stressed;
3. a model farm truck to haul grain. An overview of how gasoline powered engines operate may be emphasized;
4. samples of corn, wheat, and oats. Tests on germination may be made;
5. a model set of farm animals. Here, learners may study automation in feeding farm animals.

Pupils may study the models on the learning centre and ask questions of each other and of the teacher. Perhaps, questions such as the follow'ng are raised by pupils after viewing the models:

1. how does a self propelled combine work to cut again?
2. how is soil prepared for drilling and seeding grain?
3. what determines which grain to seed in a given field?
4. how is automation used to feed farm animals?
5. how is grain stored on the farm?

The above questions, as an example, provide a basis for pupils with teacher guidance to develop an experience chart. Ideas come from pupils pertaining to what was experienced from the learning centre. The teacher assists and guides pupils to present content for the experience chart. The teacher prints the ideas from pupils in neat manuscript letters on the chalkboard or on a transparency for overhead use. We have observed numerous teachers type the ideas presented by pupils using a word processor and a large screen to project the resulting ideas. Learners may then see their talk written down. From the concrete experiences of objects at the learning centre, pupils may see the abstract words on the large screen.

After the content has been printed/typed, pupils with teacher help may read the content together orally. The teacher needs to point to the words and phrases as they are being read. This guide pupils into becoming better readers. For some, these are beginning experiences in reading on the early primary grade levels. With the typed/printed subject matter in a transparency or in the computer, pupils may enjoy reading the same content at a later time. Rereading content is good for pupils and provides increased opportunities to develop a good stock of sight words in science. If the ideas from pupils have been printed on the chalkboard, they may be transferred to a flip chart so the content is saved and can be read later in a loosely bound volume. Sometimes pupil's ideas are printed immediately onto the flip chart. This saves the time of the teacher if this is done; however, many teachers feel they cannot immediately print the ideas correctly from pupils as they are given.

There are numerous questions that arise pertaining to the use of experience charts. Should the teacher write the ideas down directly as given orally by learners. The content may lack completeness, correct grammar, and usage. We would say that the teacher can ask for other ways to state a sentence if the one given has its many weaknesses. A short period of time for brainstorming might well provide the quality of sentences desired by the teacher of science. The experience chart may be written individually, within a cooperative learning endeavour, or the class as a whole. There are times when individual pupils have content they desire the teacher write for them. At other times the teacher may wish committee work on an experience chart so that are more chances for learner interaction within a small group. If the class size is large, the teacher may wish to have a smaller group work on an experience chart. The ideas presented by each pupil should be respected by all involved in developing the experience chart.

Closely related to experience charts approaches in science reading is the whole language programme of reading instruction. Instead of segmenting reading instruction in terms of phonics instruction and other word recognition procedures, whole language advocates advocate the wholeness of content read. It is the entire story or event that is salient. Ediger (1997) wrote the following pertaining to whole language philosophies of teaching and learning in reading:

Teachers, whom we supervise, advocating a strong whole language approach in teaching reading stress the following:

1. reading involves wholeness in that ideas are read sequentially by learners;
2. the wholeness involved in reading should not be interrupted with phonics or other word recognition techniques. Obtaining ideas, not phonics, is salient;
3. interest in reading generates motivation to learn; interest overcomes problems, in word recognition. Much reading then assists pupils to identify an increased number of words;
4. providing assistance to pupils, as needed, is sufficient for learners to recognize unknown words. This, as needed approach, also prevents pupils from fragmenting content read in reading;

5. learner enjoyment in reading needs to be whole, not segmented into parts.

Toward the other end of the continuum, student teachers and regular teachers whom we supervised believed that whole language approaches are more suited toward pupils who can read well, such as in recreational reading. These readers can sequence their very own reading materials at a personal, optimal rate of speed. Little assistance is then needed in identifying unknown words. Teachers, here, agree that selected pupils do use context clues heavily to identify unknown words. Since pupils are different one from another, it stands to reason that some pupils will be orientated toward the whole language approach...

Helping the Mainstreamed Pupil

The Education for All Handicapped Pupils law (PL 94-142) in US emphasizes that handicapped pupils be placed in the test restricted environment. Too frequently, all handicapped pupils had been placed in a special education classroom. Presently, many of these handicapped pupils are placed into the regular classroom. Here, the regular teacher teaches the handicapped together with normal children in a mainstreamed class. An IEP (individualized educational plan) is written for each pupils who is mainstreamed. The plan spells out with measurable stated objectives what a pupil is to achieve within a given interval of time. Learning activities are indicated for teachers so that they may assist pupils to achieve the IEP objectives. Auditing is possible to determine if objectives have been achieved by the mainstreamed pupil. I have served as an auditor to audit if a pupil has/has not achieved selected objectives. The auditor needs to notice if there is evidence to show that a show that a pupil was successful in goal attainment.

IDEA (Individuals with Disabilities Education Act) was passed by the United States congress and signed by the president in 1990. This law further protects the rights of handicapped pupils with a free and appropriate education.

Appropriate means that the pupil needs proper placement and assistance for those who are impaired in speech, hearing, and sight. Orthopaedically handicapped pupils also need adequate provisions made for them as do pupils with learning disabilities. Parental involvement, including placement of the disabled was also emphasized in IDEA.

In research on mainstreaming or inclusion of the handicapped into the regular classroom, Gottlieb and Leyser (1996) wrote:

The present findings revealed two primary findings. First, that parents who indicated that they had a family member with disabilities were more positive of mainstreaming in 1991 than in 1981, and second that the more positive shift in attitude was not evident for the numerically larger group of parents indicated they did not have a family member with disabilities.

From the perspectives of families that had a member with disabilities, the data suggest that the relative commonplace fact of mainstreaming, and inclusion, has reduced concerns and fears of the unknown regarding what might happen in integrated classrooms serving students with disabilities alongside their non disabled peers. For this community of families, mainstreaming seems now a more acceptable, programmatic option for all children. The magnitude of the change may be indicated as follows: for parents indicating that they have a family member with disabilities, the power of the differences in mean attitude scores between 1981 and 1991 was 1:00, with an effect size of 3:00. This represents a powerful difference in attitude scores.

Parents who did not report the presence of a family member with disabilities did not express a shift in attitudes, either in the positive or negative direction. Evidently, mainstreaming did not arouse parental concerns that their non disabled children would be negatively affected by the presence of classmates with disabilities...

The IEP protects handicapped pupils so they are not ignored in teaching and learning. There are goals that need to be achieved by these learners. The IEP's also spell out what kinds of services are to be received by each handicapped child such as speech correction for the impaired child in speaking. Teachers, the principal, and parents need to be involved in developing the IEP as well as identifying the necessary services to be provided.

The teacher of science then needs to provide for the handicapped pupil who is mainstreamed into the regular classroom.

The IEP objectives need to be met in teaching. Hopefully an aide will assist the regular teacher to provide for the mainstreamed handicapped pupil. There are no easy ways of teaching any pupil, but it mainstreamed or normal pupils. We, however, recommend the following in teaching the handicapped:

1. Determine where each pupil is achieving presently and then, based on these findings, develop an IEP. Involve teachers, the principal, parents, and the guidance counsellor in developing an appropriate IEP.
2. Provide all needed services for the handicapped, such as speech correction and ways to remedy learning disorders such as dyslexia.
3. Use learning opportunities that stimulate and encourage pupils to achieve objectives.
4. Evaluate to notice learner progress in achieving objectives.
5. Use evaluation information to improve the quality of teaching the handicapped.
6. Make certain aides have been properly instructed as to their roles in teaching handicapped pupils.
7. Discuss with parents which is better for their child, mainstreaming or being taught in a special education class.

Slow learners, in general may be guided through a variety of learning opportunities in achieving more optimally. A good reader or the teacher may read orally to these pupils as they follow along in their own science textbooks. The content read orally might then be discussed with the slow learner. These same pupils should receive practice reading the same content that was read orally. The background information as well as seeing and hearing the words pronounced accurately provides the kinds knowledge and skills needed to read on their own.

If there is teacher time, simplified content will assist the slow learner to do a better job of reading. Subject matter can always be simplified by using easier terms of context as well as sentences that are more readily understood. We have found that pupils who lack reading skills appropriate for what others are reading may select and read related library book content in science. There should be an atmosphere of respect when provisions are made for individual differences. There are so many people not able to work and achieve, is it not a blessing to be able to do more than others who are unable to do so, for various reasons? We believe most children in school want to learn much and achieve at a high level, as much as abilities permit. We believe there is an inward feeling of satisfaction with high achievement. An inadequate self concept says, "I can't do this." Or, "It is impossible for me to learn as much as others do." The self concept needs to be nurtured and supported of each pupil. Learners need to achieve success through hard work and feel they can be successful. We have found, numerous times, that there are pupils who do not learn as much as they are capable of. This hurts the self concept of the pupil. The learner is not achieving and can do better, regardless of ability levels. There is joy in achieving and learning, be in utilitarian to be used in a practical situation or in having worth for its own sake. Learning activities should be there to assist pupils to learn as much as possible on an individual basis.

In addition to reading orally as well as simplifying content for pupils in reading, the teacher also may use the experience chart idea whereby, from an experience, pupils may present the subject matter orally for the teacher to record on a chart.

Pupils then see talk written down and may then read it back to the teacher orally. This procedure is very sound. Pupils are reading their very own ideas; they have the necessary background information from personal experiences such as an excursion on the school grounds to notice sheet or gulley erosion. These learners also know and can identify words in reading since the words came from involved pupils. By saving the experience charts, pupils may read again and again, if they wish, the printed content.

The Reading Recovery Programme, brought to the United States from New Zealand, is a one on one programme of instruction. One teacher for one child can make much difference on achievement in science. Here, we recommend securing volunteers from the community to guide slow learners in reading science content. One teacher for one child should ensure for success in reading. The aide may then assist pupils in word recognition as well as read science content to the child orally. There are ways of teaching whereby all pupils may be successful in learning. With the many audio-visual materials of instruction available, where no reading is required, pupils can learn many salient concepts and generalizations in science in ongoing lessons and units of study.

Assisting the Gifted

The gifted and talented, too frequently, are left out of the spectrum in providing for individual differences. These learners also need their fair share of time with the classroom teacher. They need quality, challenging objectives, learning opportunities which truly emphasize reaching for the stars, as well as valid and reliable evaluation techniques. What might the science teacher do to assist each pupil to learn as much as possible? We would recommend individual and cooperative projects that stimulate and encourage the gifted/talented to lofty, attainable goals. A research project might then be stressed that relates to, but goes beyond regular classroom work. The research project should have a clearly stated problem. The problem is important and relevant. A variety of reference sources and activities should be used to gather information directly related to the identified problem. Pupils are clear on the reference sources to be used. The teacher needs to provide direction on available references and the use of each. The internet, along with other sources, may provide necessary information in answer to the problem. A tentative answer may then be developed. The answer here is tentative since it needs to be tested in a utilitarian way. Additional resources may be used in the testing of the answer. This may mean revising the answer, if evidence warrants. Integration of content is a key concept in using problem solving as a means of teaching and learning. Pertaining to an integrated curriculum, Harp and Brewer (1991) wrote:

A scope and sequence decision that will profoundly alter the way you teach is whether you will integrate the curriculum, by which we mean combining instructional objectives from two or more curriculum areas into one lesson or unit. We believe that teachers face an impossible task when they view each piece of the curriculum as a single building block and teaching as stacking those blocks one on to the other. There are too many curriculum blocks to build a tower successfully. In making scope and sequence decisions you need to search for ways to integrate the curriculum. Obviously, we believe that reading and writing should be taught together. Other possible combinations are music and reading, reading and art, social studies and writing and reading, and science and physical education.

We concur that reading and writing in a research project are one, not separate entities. Certainly there is much reading that gifted/talented pupils need to do as well as considerable writing in conducting research in the science curriculum.

News magazines and daily newspapers from the centralized library may provide further information sources for the gifted/talented. Pupils may read and discuss current events items in science within a cooperative learning endeavour. The teacher needs to be on the lookout for learning activities to optimalize learning for the gifted/talented. Ediger (1984) wrote:

A quality teacher is a proficient evaluator of learner progress. A variety of appraisal procedures need to be utilized. Among other evaluation techniques, the following may be utilized:

1. Teacher observation.
2. Anecdotal records.
3. Sociometric devices.
4. Teacher written tests.
5. Checklists and rating scales.
6. Standardized achievement tests.
7. Personality tests.
8. Interest inventories.
9. Criterion referenced tests.
10. Self-evaluation by the learner.

In Summary

There are numerous means available to guide pupils to achieve more optimally in reading in science. The teacher should assist pupil in word recognition in context. This is a powerful way to have learners recognize unknown words. At the same time, recognizing words in context does not hinder in securing sequential ideas while reading. Reading science content then needs to be as holistic as possible. However, teachers must be available at teachable moments whereby analyzing words may be highly beneficial to pupils. Thus a small amount of time, as needed, may be given by the teacher to guide learners in phonics or syllabication. By giving time in analyzing unknown words, the teacher is helping pupils to develop a wider array of sight words. Reading fluently and in a manner stressing diverse approaches in comprehension is an ultimate goal in reading in science. Basal texts may be wisely used as a part of the science curriculum, but this does not, by any means, stress the entire unit of study. It is one learning activity among many others. Learners need to use content from science textbooks to identify and solve problems. The basal textbooks might also be used to check hypotheses and in their revision. If textbooks have a quality manual section, this aids the teacher in selecting objectives, learning opportunities, and evaluation techniques. Suggestions for improving teaching should always be welcomed by the teacher.

Basal science textbooks may be used to guide pupils in securing needed facts, concepts, and generalizations within the framework of problem solving. Higher levels of cognition should be stressed in the science curriculum. Certainly, a good teacher is not satisfied with pupils achieving facts only or largely, but has pupils move in the direction of thinking critically and creatively about content being pursued. Individual differences need to be provided for in reading content in science. Ediger (1997) wrote the following for a quality programme of reading instruction in the science curriculum:

1. Each pupil begins at a point where he/she is ready to achieve as optimally as possible.
2. The learner experiences continual progress successfully in reading.
3. The four vocabularies—listening, speaking, reading and writing—are integrated into a quality reading programme.
4. Word recognition skills, such as phonics, syllabication, context clues, and structural analysis, are taught within a framework of interesting content to be read.
5. Major emphasis placed upon reading literature, not analyzing words into component parts.
6. Multimedia approaches are used to motivate pupils so that an inward desire in learning to read is inherent.
7. Problem solving, critical and creative thinking, as well as application of salient concepts stressed in teaching reading.
8. The best sequences is used to guide each pupil toward optimum achievement in reading.
9. Learning to read as a lifetime endeavour is stressed.
10. The use of relevant research results is important in the teaching of reading.

REFERENCES

Barr, Rebecca, and Marilyn Sadow (1985). *Reading Diagnosis for Teachers*. White Plains, New York: Longman Inc., Page. 143.

Cagney, George, and Christine Neuenfeld (1993), "Teacher's Preference for Reading Materians," *Reading Improvement*, Vol. 30, No. 4, Page 244.

Carlo, Marie (1996), "Recorded Books Raise Reading Scores," *The Education Digest*, Vol. 61, Page 56.

Ediger, Marlow (1984), "Goals in the Reading Curriculum," *Reading Improvement*, Vol. 21, No. 3, Page 243.

Ediger, Marlow (1996). *Elementary Education*. Kirksville, Missouri: Simpson Publishing Company, Page 39.

Ediger, Marlow (1997). *Teaching Reading and the Language Arts in the Elementary School*. Kirksville, Missouri: Simpson Publishing Company, Page 37.

Ediger, Marlow (1997). *Teaching Reading and the Language Arts in the Elementary School*. Kirksville: Simpson Publishing Company, Page 24.

Harp, Bill, and Jo Ann Brewer (1991). *Reading and Writing: Teaching for the Connections*. New York: Harcourt Brace and Jovanovich, Publishers, Page 98.

Harris, Albert J., and Edward Sipay (1985). *How to Increase Reading Ability*. White Plains, New York: Longman Inc. Page 504.

Gottlieb, Jay, and Yona Leyser (1996), "Attitudes of Public School Parents Toward Mainstreaming Changes Over a Decade." *Journal of Instructional Psychology*, Vol. 23, No. 4, Pages 263.

Mc Ninch, George W., and Ellen Gruber (1996), "Perceptions of Literacy Acquisition (Traditionals Vs. Whole Language): Teachers, Principals, and Parents," *Reading Improvement*, Vol. 33, No. 3, Pages 130-136.

Ruben, Dorothy (1983). *Teaching Reading and Study Skills in Content Areas*. New York: Rinehart and Winston, Pages 109-110.

13

Affective Objectives in the Science Curriculum

Science teachers need to stress three kinds of objectives in teaching and learning. The first kind, cognitive, does receive major emphasis by teachers. Cognitive goals stress pupils achieving well in acquiring vital facts in ongoing lessons and units of study. There are selected educators in science who tend to down play the importance of vital facts that learners are to achieve. Perhaps the problem here is more of what is done with the facts as compared to saying that pupils achieving factual information is evil. Facts are the building blocks of developing concepts. Concepts are broader than facts and may contain many facts in each concept. Consider the following fact: there are three major kinds of rock-igneous, metamorphic, and sedimentary. We believe this is a valuable fact for pupils to achieve in a unit on "Rocks and Minerals." The term 'igneous' is a concept. Many facts are contained therein, such as

1. Igneous rock comes from the interior of the earth where temperature readings are very high.
2. Molten rock is made of magma and lava.
3. The molten rock comes through fissures in the earth.

In addition to vital facts and concepts, pupils should also acquire major generalizations. Generalizations in science relate several concepts into a declarative sentence. The following is a generalization:

Common forms of igneous rock are granite used for tombstones, pumice used in building materials, and obsidian used in making decorative items. The concepts here are igneous rock, granite, tombstones, pumice, building materials, obsidian, and decorative items.

In addition to facts, concepts, and generalizations, pupils also need to be able to think critically. When pupils, for example, make comparisons among igneous, metamorphic, and sedimentary rocks, critical thinking is involved. When pupils brainstorm the many uses of rock and think of unique uses also, then creative thought is in evidence. Going one notch higher in cognitive objectives, if pupils engage in problem solving, they need to identify a problem, gather information in answer to the question or problem, and test the information in a utilitarian situation. The following are examples of identified problems:

1. Why does the interior of the earth continually become hotter the further one goes inside the surface?
2. What causes volcanic eruptions?

Cognitive objectives are salient for pupils to achieve in ongoing lessons and units of study. Thus there is much knowledge that a pupil needs to acquire as well as use the knowledge in a practical way in society. Related to cognitive objectives are affective ends for pupil attainment.

Affective Objectives in Science

Affective objectives involve attitudes, feelings, emotions, and beliefs. There are several relatively new programmes in science education that stress the emotions and their consequences for individuals. We have noticed several of my student teachers and supervising or cooperating teachers, called a teaching team, whom we supervised in the public schools who stress much pupil involven ent in the science curriculum. These teachers emphasize rather heavy pupil involvement in curriculum development. In several situations these teaching teams had worked out a set of learning centres whereby pupils individually could choose which tasks to pursue and which to omit in an ongoing science unit of study. Learners might then sequence their very own experiences in the ongoing science unit of study. We will describe one set of centres one of us observed in which the unit of study in science was entitled. "The Changing Surface of the Earth".

The following learning centres were then in evidence:

1. a soil erosion centre;
2. folding and faults in and on the earth's surface
3. flood damage in an area centre;
4. contours, strip cropping, terracing, and planted grass/ trees to avoid erosion;
5. wind and water erosion;
6. the weathering process, including freezing and thawing;
7. pollution of the natural environment;
8. saving forest regions;
9. mining for rocks and minerals in a responsible manner;
10. use of natural resources responsibly.

Each centre had concrete (real objects and items), semiconcrete (audiovisual aids), and abstract materials of instruction (cassettes, reading materials, written work, discussions and other oral communication activities). There were four to five tasks per learning centre for pupils to select to work on. For example, centre #2 above had the following tasks on a task card:

1. By using reference material at this centre, find causes for both folding and faulting.
2. Using the modelling materials, make a model of folding and of faulting and faulting in and on the planet earth.
3. Prepare an oral report on folding and faulting to be presented to the entire class.

4. Make drawings of folding and faulting for display on walls in the hallway.
5. What happens to lives and property when severe faults cause problems?

Pupils at these learning centres make many decisions, such as which tasks to pursue sequentially. Teachers are guides and encourage as well as assist pupils to achieve continually. The pupil then chooses which tasks to complete and which to omit. The choices are made based on purpose possessed by each pupil. Then too, there are ample opportunities for pupils to work collaboratively if they so desire. There are activity centred tasks as well as those that require or stress more of abstract endeavours. The learning style of individual pupils are involved in making decisions. The teacher does not dictate nor lecture what pupils are to learn. The interests of pupils are salient in learner centred instruction. Thus the attitudinal dimension of the learner is paramount in an affective centred science curriculum. The feelings and emotions are involved here in decisions made. The pupil also assists in evaluating his/her own progress in products and processes of learning.

Emotional Intelligence

There are an increasing number of educators who advocate the feeling dimension in learning. Pool (1997) summarizes key ideas presented by Dan Goleman (1995) who wrote *Emotional Intelligence* and speaks frequently at educational conventions; these main ideas follow. According to Goleman, there are five dimensions of emotional intelligence. First is self awareness. Here, pupil realize increasingly so that there are personal strengths and weaknesses and use these to become decisive in decision making. Understanding their very own feelings is important so that action options are more prevalent. Self confidence is very important in order to make choices and act to make decisions.

Second, pupils need to learn to handle their emotions. Impulsive behaviour may make for incorrect decisions.

Learners need to develop more of a *wait* approach so that options may be scrutinized in terms of advantages and disadvantages. The consequences of each choice need to be assessed. Being impulsive might well lead to improper ends in life. Third, learners need to feel motivated in achieving definite goals. Hope is involved in having these goals in life. The motivation then comes from diverse goals that an individual aims for. Optimism is necessary to achieve and reach objectives one has in mind. Fourth, empathy is very important for pupils to develop. Feeling of empathy make possible to sympathize with others. Empathy is learned. Thus one learns to assist others in positive ways or be brutal to others. Compassion for others is important. Fifth, the development of social skills enables a pupil to help others in every day situations in life. Politeness and friendliness enable a person to interact well with others in society on a daily basis.

Emotional intelligence harmonizes well with an affective science curriculum. Thus with pupil/teacher planning of the curriculum, self awareness is developed increasingly so when pupils select the order of learning activities in science. Strengths in decision making should be an end result. When pupils learn to handle emotions, there is persistence and effort put forth in learning. The immediate goal is not what is necessarily good such as impulsive behaviour. Rather the pupil needs to evaluate the pros and cons in making choices. Motivation is necessary in order that goals are achieved by pupils in science. With the absence of goals, energy levels for learning go downhill.

Feelings of empathy make it possible for pupils individually to get along well with others. In school and in society, it is necessary to have good human relations so that achievement and group efforts are possible. Human beings are feeling individuals, not automatons. Social skills need learning by pupils so that a friendly and considerate environment is available for all to achieve more optimally. Committee endeavours in ongoing lessons and units of study in science provide many opportunities for pupils to develop social skills.

Pertaining to humanism as a psychology of education, Woolfolk and Nicolich (1990) wrote:

> Humanistic interpretations of motivation emphasize personal freedom, choice, self-determination, and striving for personal growth, or as A.H. Maslow (1954) called it, self-actualization. With these emphases, the humanistic psychologists tend to be in harmony with many of the constructivist approaches. Perhaps most important is the fact that both views stress intrinsic motivation.

Shepherd and Ragan (1982) outline a summary of A.H. Maslow's (1954) hierarcy of human needs or goals as follows:

1. Physiological—a need to survive
   A. Homeostasis—a balance of internal bodily functions
   B. Appetites—need for nurture-food, sleep, air, elimination...
2. Safety—freedom from damage and threat
   A. Routines and Rules (know and accept)
   B. Consistency and security...
3. Belongingness—need for love and affection...
   A. Intimate relations with other people
   B. To be accepted, wanted, and cherished...
4. Esteem—status, recognition, competence, importance, independence
   A. Personal-need for strength, mastery
   B. Group—reputation, status, dominance, appreciation...
5. Self-Actualization
   A. To satisfy potential—you must be what you can be...

In our own experiences as teacher educator including supervising student teachers and cooperating teachers for several years, we believe affective and cognitive objectives interact. It is difficult to separate the two categories of goals. Thus when we speak at conventions for teacher education and write for publication, we stress that quality emotions and feelings assist pupils to achieve at a more optimal rate in the cognitive domain. Our observations of pupils in the public schools indicate that individuals who are hostile, negative, have short attention spans, and mistreat others in the classroom have a difficult time to achieve what their potential is, much more so than other pupils in the class setting. Thus quality attitudes in the affective dimension assist learners to achieve more optimally in the cognitive area.

Humanists desire open ended or general objectives, rather than measurably written or behaviourally stated objectives for pupils to achieve. Why? Not all pupils, by any means, learn the same things due to choices and decisions made by pupils in ongoing units of study (see learning centres above for examples). If teachers determine objectives for all pupils to achieve in science units of study, there is no room for learners to select and omit selected learning opportunities, based on learner perceived purposes. If pupils select sequential objectives to achieve, within a flexible framework, a psychological sequence is involved as compared to a logical order whereby the teacher arranges the order of objectives for pupil attainment. Sequence resides within the learner, not within the minds of teachers or textbooks in science. Formal means of teaching here are eliminated and replaced with learner choices and decisions as to what to learn and what to omit. The feeling, affective dimension is definitely involved in making choices and decisions. (Ediger, 1996).

A pupil centred curriculum might be emphasized, in part through individualized reading in science. Thus instead of using basal textbooks in science units, pupils may choose to read library books that related directly to the unit title being situated. In a unit on "The Changing Surface of the Earth", an adequate number of library books on different reading levels need to be available for pupil choice. I have observed this approach to be very successful in ongoing lessons and units of study. Pupils then relate what was read from a library book read to the ensuing discussion. There appears to be much discussion and excitement when this approach is used in teaching science. Pupils might then notice different points of view expressed which can lead to analysis and evaluation of subject matter read.

In addition to pupils choosing sequential library books to read and relating the content to ongoing discussions, the science teacher might also have conferences with individual pupils or several pupils who have read the same library book where multiple copies of a book were available. Here, the teacher might observe pupil enthusiasm, interest, and quality of comprehension. The science teacher can always diagnose strengths and weaknesses shown by pupils in the conference setting. What has been diagnosed as weaknesses might then be remediated through additional learning activities. (Ediger, 1997). Pupil choices in the science curriculum might be made in whole or in part. The latter might be stressed in individualized reading in science which then substitutes for the basal textbook in ongoing units of study.

Democracy in the Science Curriculum

Democracy as a way of life emphasizes that pupils respect each other's ideas and contributions. Ridiculing and minimizing others has no role to play in democratic situations. Pupils should achieve more optimally when democracy as a way of life is practised.

Fenstermacher (1996) wrote:

We hear a great deal about readying the next generation of workers for global competition... about world class standards for what is learned in school. We here almost nothing about building civic participation or building and maintaining democratic communities, whether these be neighbourhoods or governments at the local, state or federal levels. The advancement of democratic ideals and institutions goes largely unmentioned, taken for granted or insufficiently important to rank up there with such world shaking events as or playing Avis to Japan's Hertz.

Pupils discussing current events items in science provide excellent opportunities for learners to practice tenets of democratic living within a committee endeavour. In one of my classroom observations, student teachers and cooperating teachers orientated learners in the classroom to bring from the home setting current events items pertaining to natural disasters. These natural disasters included tornadoes, hail, volcanic eruptions, floods, strong winds, heavy snow, and ice storms, among others. News items could deal with different times of the year. The clippings were brought to class for discussion within a committee endeavour. A large world map was placed at the centre of a bulletin board. Yarn was used to connect the happening from the news clipping with the place of occurrence, located on the world map.

We have observed numerous student teachers and cooperating teachers whom we have supervised stressing democracy in the classroom with cooperative learning endeavours. These teachers have developed standards with pupils in terms of how a committee should function. The following were developed as standards for a committee, with teacher guidance, to work by in discussing current events in science:

1. respect each other and the thinking of others;
2. listen carefully to the thinking of committee members as ideas are being presented;
3. have all pupils participate in discussing current events in science within the committee;
4. let leadership emerge as the discussion moves forward;
5. ask questions if comments made are not clear;
6. do not interrupt when others are participating.

These criteria were posted in the classroom and reviewed with learners prior to each committee working in the area of discussing current events in science. After committee work, members with teacher guidance evaluated how well the group had followed each criteria. It appears that reviewing with pupils the meaning of each standard and appraising if individual standards are being met is helpful to learners. Pupils can be taught democratic tenets as a way of life. Pupil achievement hinges on being able to accept others more fully and not reveal animosity or ill will toward others. Positive attitudes toward others enhances the individual to achieve more optimally in the cognitive domain as well as make for better feelings about the self. Pupils seemingly quarrel less and assist each other more when healthy self concepts and emotional well being are in evidence.

Conclusion

The emotions, feelings, and values are important parts of an individual's well being and achievement in life. Science teachers should emphasize an adequate number of objectives stressing the affective domain. Actually, the affective domain cannot be separated from the cognitive. If pupils possess quality attitudes, the chances are the rest will be achieved well in life as much as the individual is capable.

REFERENCES

Ediger, Marlow (1996), *Elementary Education* (Kirksville, Missouri: Simpson Publishing Company), 134.

Ediger, Marlow (1997), *Teaching Reading and the Language Arts in the Elementary School* (Kirksville, Missouri: Simpson Publishing Company) 32.

Fenstermacher, Gary D. (1995), "The Absence of Democratic and Educational Ideals from Contemporary Educational Reform Initiatives," *Educational Horizons*, 73: 70.

Goleman, Daniel (1995), *Emotional Intelligence* (New York: Bantam Books).

Maslow, A.H. (1954), *Motivation and Personality* (New York): Harper and Row.

Shepherd, Gene., and William B. Ragan (1982), *Modern Elementary Curriculum* (New York): Holt, Rinehart and Winston, 15.

Woolfolk, Anita, and Lorraine Mc Cune Nicolich (1990), *Educational Psychologies for Teachers* (Englewood Cliffs), New Jersey: Prentice-Hall, Inc, 321.

Pool, Carolyn R. (1997), "Up with Emotional Health," *Educational Leadership*, 54, 8: 12-14.

14

When Pupils Fail, Then What?

Much is written about avoiding pupil failure in school and having an increased number graduate from high school, than the present seventy-five per cent rate. The probably is no other institution, other than the public schools, whereby so many pupils are to attend the same institution and go through a similar curriculum, especially the elementary and middle school years of schooling. The high school level provides more opportunities for pupils to differentiate in terms of courses taken, such as electives in the curriculum as compared to the elementary school. Or a pupil on the secondary level may go the vocational rather than the academic route. It appears, however, that the academic route is considered much superior as compared to the vocational route. We do not believe that it should be perceived this way. Rather, individuals are different from each other in many ways and selected pupils will feel more empowered in vocational as compared to academic classes. Society certainly does need its vocational people to do carpenter work, repair automobiles, prepare food in restaurants, do plumbing, and the myriads of needed employment in society.

Voucher Systems

There are educators and people from the business, world who advocate that schools which fail pupils should provide vouchers to parents to choose a receiving school for their child. Here, Parents need to be very receptive in studying what different schools have to offer in meeting individual needs of pupils. Receiving schools need to publish brochures to indicate what they have to offer incoming pupils. They should make known what it is that would assist pupils to do well in school. Dissatisfied parents may have behaviourally disordered children and need a school for their children that can offer a necessary curriculum. We would venture to speculate that pupils who do not do well in school, according to parental expectations, may have special needs. These pupils have not done well in the sending schools and now are looking for greener pastures where all is well. This may or may not follow when a pupil under the voucher system changes schools. Then too, if there are many vouchers available, will receiving schools be able to provide for pupils whose needs were not met in the sending school? If there truly is an outstanding teacher, known to many that he/she can help many pupils to be successful, how many new pupils can he/she take from receiving schools? Will the receiving school have adequate assistance for this excellent teacher to handle the new pupils? Or will the new pupils provide a burden to the outstanding teacher so that he/she can no longer do an excellent job of teaching. It takes one child who has many emotional problems to disrupt an entire classroom continuously. Then too, if the parents of this child are highly verbal in voicing dissatisfaction in the receiving school, what is the next alternative? A highly vocal parent can do much to hinder teachers in providing for individual pupils. In the US or India, if pupils do not achieve up to what newsreporters or the lay public wants in terms of test results, teachers are to blame in whole. It almost appears as if pupils have no responsibilities for achieving unless they have an inward desire to do so.

What if parents do not have the money to pay for differences between what the receiving school asks for in terms of money and what the sending school offers? There can be quite a gap between the two in dollars. Then too, transportation can be a real problem in sending a pupil to a different school. Will parents have the money and time to take their child to a different school? Schools also need to be chosen on the basis of what will truly assist a child to do better. This can be a major problem in selecting a new school for a pupil to attend under the voucher system. This opens the doors to a touchy situation in that some parents would choose parochial schools for their children. Would it be constitutional to send a child to a parochial school from voucher moneys? If too many pupils with parental approval decide to attend parochial schools and if this were legal, the parochial system of instruction would change much. Special services for the handicapped would need to be provided. All pupils who wished to do so may have to be admitted to the chosen parochial school. The role of the state might involve supervising parochial schools in term of teachers hired and the quality of the curriculum offered. Parochial schools might then need to be enlarged with a problem arising as to who would pay for these costs.

We have the following questions to ask about the voucher system of parental choice of schools for their children, in addition to the problems raised above:

1. Will the quality of education really improve for the pupil with the voucher system?
2. Why not spend the voucher money, instead, in improving all public schools in the US?
3. How are brochures developed by receiving schools presenting their data in terms of honesty, objectivity, and integrity?
4. What happens to receiving schools when receiving vouchers to admit pupils in terms of school size, class size, and quality of instruction?
5. What happens to a pupil who no longer attends the neighourhood school in terms of feelings and friendships left behind?

Open Enrolment

There are several states, such as Minnesota and Iowa, that have open enrolment. With open enrolment, parents may choose which school in the state their child is to attain. The neighbourhood school might, of course, then be bypassed. The local school is not as certain how many pupils they will have at the beginning of the school year since the option is open in terms of which school the pupil will be attending. Parents may then select a school based on the kind of curriculum which will be offered to their child. There is no money available in terms of vouchers to pay for changing from one public school to another. Parents need to find out then which school might offer a curriculum that would be of benefit to their children.

Feelings of insecurity may be there when a public school does not know how many pupils will be at the beginning of a school year. The same would be true of any receiving school. A problem then of space for pupils and adequate teachers need to be considered by the receiving schools. Many times, educators and the lay public argue that poor quality schools will be eliminated with open enrolment plans. Thus schools offering poor quality education may eventually have too few pupils to operate an educational system.

We have the following questions to raise about open enrolment:

1. Do parents select schools based on quality or rather on slogans presented? In other words are there ulterior motives in making choices of schools such as a boy or girl desiring to play on a basketball/football team which is known for its winning record and possible scholarships? Perhaps, there is nothing wrong in wanting to be on a top team in competitive athletics in order to obtain a scholarship. For example, we do have the theory of multiple intelligences which includes bodily/kinesthetic intelligence.
2. Why not attempt to improve all public schools so that diverse curricula are offered within each school to provide for individual differences among pupils?

3. How can parents know which school will meet the needs of their children best?
4. Does a receiving school with a good track record want to accept numerous other pupils and perhaps ruin their good reputation due to having too many pupils or to many disruptive pupils?
5. Is it best for a local district to know approximately how many pupils there will be at the beginning of a school year in order to make quality plans for instruction?

Measuring Pupil Achievement

There are many ways to measure pupil achievement including standardized norm referenced tests, criterion referenced tests, districtwide tests, state mandated tests, tests which accompany a basal reading or mathematics series, Education 2000 goals with diverse states developing tests to measure pupil achievement in attainment of stated objectives, national tests such as the National Assessment of Educational Progress (NAEP), and international tests which makes comparisons of pupil achievement among nations on the planet earth. We do not think educators and the lay public understand how each test is devised and why there is so much controversy about how to measure pupil achievement and progress.

A. Standardized Tests. There are many rules which need to be followed before a test is standardized. A standardized test has the same directions to follow for all taking the test. The time limits are the same for all regardless of ability and achievement levels of pupils involved, scoring procedures of the results are the same, among other standardizations. The results of our pupils having taken the test are compared with those of the group the test was standardized on in numerous pilot studies. The manual section of the standardized test will state which categories of pupils were included in the standardization group.

We see the following as major weakrresses of standardized testing to indicate pupil progress:

1. there are no objectives that go along with these kinds of tests. The teacher then cannot teach so that pupils might achieve objectives. Guesswork is involved in terms of what the test is to measure. What the teacher teaches is then not valid in terms of content in test items on the standardized test;
2. pupils lack security in not knowing what they will be tested on. What has been studied might be completely unrelated to content in the test items;
3. a test such as standardized tests may have high reliability and yet validity is difficult to determine. To be valid a test must measure what it purports to measure and that is pupil achievement in the different curriculum or academic areas. What is taught by teachers varies much from school to school. In a national curriculum, pupils could be studying similar things in each of the different curriculum areas. That is something, however, that would not be prized in the US, at least not now. Thus there are no common objectives in and on standardized tests that teachers should teach for so that pupils might be successful in goal attainment. In addition to validity, reliability is an important term in testing and evaluation. It is much easier in pilot studies to obtain statistical figures on reliability. Reliability stresses consistency of test results for pupils when a retest or split-half reliability is used. Thus the chances are if a test item is written clearly, the pupil will respond consistently when the same test is being given such as in test-retest reliability. From pilot studies in standardizing a test, weak items can be eliminated or modified so that consistency in terms of pupils' responses is obtained.

B. Criterion referenced tests. Here, the teacher has relatively easy access to the objectives that need emphasis in teaching so that he/she may stress selected subject matter in teaching learners. The test items then might be quite valid for pupils if the teacher has aligned instruction with the stated objectives. The content taught may then be valid since it aligns with the objectives. Reliability might also be good if the results from the CRT are the same/similar from pupils in a test/retest situation.

Our reservations about CRTs include the following:

1. the developers of the CRTs did not run pilot studies on test results of pupils; thus there is no data to show the validity and reliability of the CRT. In fact, this has happened in selected states in the US. The governor of a state then wished to hurry with implementing a new CRT and did not have educators do statistical analysis of pupil test results;
2. CRT tend to have too many factual test items rather than stressing pupils engaging in critical and creative thinking as well as problem solving. Generally with multiple choice test items, the trend would be for factual knowledge to dominate content in and on the test;
3. districtwide tests. These tests are developed in the same way as is true of CRTs. Districtwide tests, however, are written by teachers and administrators on the local school district level as compared to the state level as was true of CRTs. Unless carefully developed districtwide tests might have the same weaknesses as do CRTs. It costs money and takes time to run tests of validity and reliability in pilot studies. However unless these pilot studies are run, the tests might well have weak and unclear test items. There are ample opportunities in districtwide tests to align with content taught by teachers within that district.

D. Test which accompany a basal mathematics textbook series or other academic area. Here, we will discuss mathematics only and accompanying tests with the basal text. There are several series that have tests inside the basal which the teacher can give to pupils. The tests seem to be well aligned, in most cares, with content covered for each unit of study in the basal. Authors of the text and the accompanying tests advocate pupils be given the test prior to teaching the first unit, for example. If a pupil obtains a score of eighty per cent or higher on the unit being pretested, he/she need not study that unit, but can take the pretest for the next unit of study in the basal. Again, if a score of eighty per cent or higher is secured by the pupil taking the pretest, he/she need not study or do the work in that unit of study. This approach of passing out of a unit continues until a pupil does not get eighty per cent or higher of the test items correct on a pretest.

We see the following weaknesses on a basal textbook test to measure pupil achievement:

1. these tests seemingly are not that valid and reliable to have pupils test out of studying and doing the work within a unit of study. We have heard most teachers of science in graduate classes as well as cooperating teachers whom we supervise in the schools make statements that doubt the strengths of using these tests to measure if pupils can test out of a unit of study. However, teachers do say pretests such as those related directly to a textbook have their strengths to offer assistance to teachers in teaching pupils. Thus what pupils miss on these pretests may become a part of objectives to achieve in the science curriculum;
2. science contains more exact and precise knowledge as compared to such curriculum areas as reading and literature, art, music, physical education, and social studies when ascertaining learner progress. We believe that science tests due to their objective content can do a better job of measuring pupil progress as compared to other academic disciplines. There still as a problem as to what to emphasize on these tests such as products versus processes, the practical as compared to the theoretical in mathematics.
3. face validity may be fairly strong in subject matter tests since the writers of the tests look at content

taught and then arrange items there from for the test. However, predictive validity is desired since the results form a learner in having taken the test is to predict how well he/she will do on the next ensuing unit of study;

4. are there selected countries in the world whose pupils do better on international tests of comparison due to classroom work in mathematics stressing more of what is covered on these tests?

5. which pupils are tested in the different nations when international comparisons are made? For example, US and India educate all pupils regardless of handicaps possessed such as mental retardation and those with behavioural disorders. Are these pupils a part of US or Indian pupils being tested and compared with other nations who do not have these kinds of learners in the comparison pool? If more of the cream of the crop of pupils are tested in a nation, then higher achievement is possible here;

6. are there too many variables among nations when making comparisons in science and mathematics achievement? For example, it is very difficult to make comparisons among nations as to how money earmarked for school is spent. In the US and India much of school money goes to busing pupils from rural areas into school. A considerable amount of money is spent also on busing for integration of the races purposes. There are nations that do not even have school buses such as Russia.

Constructivism and Evaluation

Constructivism emphasizes pupils being evaluated in terms of the situations they are in. For example, if pupils write a get well card to an ill classmate, there is a need for a writing activity. When the get well card is written, then there should be efforts made to appraise the quality of the card that will be sent to the ill classmate. Or, if a committee of pupils is doing a science experiment that relates directly to the ongoing unit, the quality of the experiment needs appraising in terms of desired criteria. It is very difficult, for example, to write a paper/pencil test item or items covering how well a science experiment was done.

Pertaining to two versions of constructivism, Alrasian and Walsh (1997) wrote:

These fundamental agreements among the constructivists are tempered by some important areas of difference about the process of constructing knowledge. These differences are reflected in two versions of cognition: developmental and socio-cultural.

Developmental theories, such as Piaget's, represent a more traditional constructivist framework. This major emphasis is on the universal forms of structures of knowledge (e.g., prelogical, concrete, and abstract operations) that guide the making of meaning. These universal cognitive structures are assumed to be developed and organised, so that prelogical thinking occurs prior to concrete logical thinking in a developmental sequence. Within this framework, the individual student is considered to be the meaning maker, with the development of the individual's personal knowledge being the main goal of learning. Critics of developmental theories of cognition point out that this perspective does not take into account "how issues such as the cultural and political nature of schooling and the race, class, and gender backgrounds of teachers and students, as well as their prior learning histories, influence the kinds of meaning that are made in the classrooms." Cognitive developmental theories, it is claimed, divorce meaning from affect by focusing on isolating universal forms of knowledge and thus limiting consideration of the socio-cultural and contextual influence on the construction of knowledge.

Constructivism then stresses the following:

1. pupils being evaluated in terms of how well they perform within a specific ongoing learning activity;

2. pupils indicating they can apply what has been learned within a relevant task;
3. pupils indicating what has been learned in an intrinsic situation such as an experience that is being stressed presently, not in a formal testing situation extrinsic to the tasks being pursued;
4. pupils perceiving the value of the activity being pursued and revealing strengths and weaknesses therein.

Additional Tests Being Advocated

It appears that schools and education of pupils is criticized all over the world (The Educational Review, 1997), Kakkar wrote on "Crisis in Education in India."

What the school, of late, has been doing sometimes makes people talk of deschooling education and foreseeing a future in which there may be no school at all. This will not happen. But there is certainly ahead of us an interval of rethinking fundamentals, and of raising schools different from the ones we have.

Education is not only in a crisis just because the school is suddenly doing worse. In fact, it has done a terribly poor job all along. But what we have been tolerating in the past we can no longer tolerate today. It is a sheer delusion to think that school has been a place that children loved, that school years are years of happiness, or that students learned a great deal in school. School in fact, has been a place of misery, of boredom, of suffering, where, as every teacher knows, only one of every fifteen students learned anything, if at all. Even college students around the turn of the century cannot expect to learn much. They go to college because they have nothing else to do, or because it leads to a professional career, or because it is the socially accepted thing to do, to make valuable connections.

There have been very vocal critics of education over the decades. Illich (1972) came out with his book on *De-Schooling*

Society. He recommended a thorough doing away with public education and offered a plan of schooling whereby arrangement would be made between a master in a field of specialization and the pupil wanting to learn what the specialist had to offer. The specialist may offer classes in the following areas: music, art, drama, literature, geography, history, the sciences, and so on. Illich believed that compulsory school attendance made for mediocrity and dehumanized education.

Too frequently, slogans in society are given to justify the thinking of the one presenting the diverse slogans (Ediger, 1997), such as in the following:

"let's have the business world teach pupils; the public schools are not doing the job." Additional slogans here could be, "The private sector has always been able to do things better than the public sector. Thus performance contracting has been emphasized in selected schools in which a certain level of achievement is guaranteed by the contractor in return for payment on a per pupil basis. Educational Alternatives of Minneapolis, Minnesota is involved in teaching pupils on a business basis. Performance contractors desire to make profits, large profits if possible for their ventures which is teaching in this case. Performance contracting was emphasized in selected school systems in the early 1970s.

Commentaries and reports on education can be quite critical. How accurate are these writings? It is hard to say. We believe a rational question might be raised about how much better other institutions in society are doing as compared to the educational arenas. There are many slogans which abound in American society.

There are groups such as the National Alliance of Business (NAB), USA who have felt that public school pupils definitely are not achieving adequately. They have offered to write tests which would demonstrate to the lay public what is lacking and needs to be changed in the public schools after viewing the test results. These approaches would involve a tremendous change in American school policy if this were done. Why? The business world of free enterprise might then determine what is of value and should be taught in the public schools. There are other segments of the population such as labour that would not be represented in such a venture. Questions that need to be raised here pertain to the following:

1. How can the business world know which content should appear on tests?
2. Is there more to the education of children other than business interests?
3. What would be the rationale of having the business world be involved in testing pupils in the public schools?
4. How does the business world train their employees at the work place; is there a model for their advocacy in the educational arena?

In addition to the business world and their plans of action, there are governmental leases who come up with ideas in education and the public schools.

Action by governmental leaders can be excellent in order to focus on the importance of education and the public schools. There are definite questions that might be raised here pertaining to additional testing and the writing of new tests such as testing fourth grades on reading achievement and eighth grades on mathematics progress:

1. Are sufficient tests available already to measure pupil achievement academically without writing new tests?
2. How will new tests be developed to stress validity in reading? There are many issues involved in reading such as phonics versus the whole language approach.
3. How much testing of pupils should be emphasized to determine achievement? Here we come up with the debate of testing versus constructivism to indicate learner progress in teaching and learning situations.
4. How do test results of pupils in a single testing situation differ from learners revealing everyday

progress in the classroom, as observed by teachers, in revealing reading achievement.

5. Who will be involved in writing test items so that politics is minimized to indicate pupil achievement in the public schools?

Conclusion

If pupils fail, then what? There are so many alternatives here that may be discussed. First of all, is the result of failure internal in that the pupil does nor care, nor put forth effort? Or, do pupils fail due to the numerous variables inherent in the public school system? Numerous approaches are used to assist pupils to do better in a receiving school such as would be true of the voucher system. Here, parents may choose which school their child is to attend, with the money available that would equal to what the sending school spends per pupil. The receiving school may spend more money per child and thus the parent needs to make up the difference plus transportation costs. Sending pupils at public expense to denominational schools is still not in evidence since church and state separation regulations apply in most cases. Open enrolment is available where by parents may select the school for the child to attend. Parents need to be aware of the curricular offerings in a new school chosen. The objectives, learning opportunities, and evaluation procedures need to harmonize with the pupil's very own style of learning. This would be true of all plans open to parents to assist the pupil to achieve and avoid failure. There may be problems involved when parents select a school away from home base for their child to attend. There may be room and board costs when the pupil is living away from home. Then too, the child may not be close to home when there is such a need to be near to parents/guardians.

Measuring up to predermined standards can be difficult for many pupils. Standardized tests do not have these predetermined standards; however, different school districts may be using these kinds of tests to measure learner progress within a given school year. A slow learner may achieve at a low level on a standardized test and yet be achieving as well as can be expected. A gifted/talented pupil may achieve at a high level on the standardized test but is not really applying himself/herself in teaching and learning situations.

CRTS can be excellent if higher levels of cognition are being measured for pupils to attain. Learners may also progress as rapidly as possible on each of the sequential objectives with provisions then being made for individual differences. Slow learners here need additional assistance to achieve as optimally as possible. Districtwide achievement tests operate in a similar manner as do CRTs. Both need to be valid and measure in terms of what pupils have had opportunities to learn in the school curriculum. If the test items are vague and poorly written, learner achievement will not be indicated in an appropriate way.

Tests based on the basal textbook being used can be one way to appraise learner progress. That is true of all valid and reliable evaluation techniques in that each procedure is an approach to determine what a pupil has learned. There are no perfect ways nor panaceas to appraise pupil achievement. The teacher needs to use a variety of techniques to determine what pupils have learned.

The National Assessment of Educational Progress (NEAP), for example, tests a random sampling of pupils in the US to ascertain what has been achieved. This is a complex venture in that the test items can not be valid for pupils to achieve. Thus there is no alignment between objectives of which there are none listed for pupils to achieve on the NAEP and the evolution items for that test. It would indeed be difficult for test writers in writing items that are to represent that which pupils have learned and achieved. The following questions arise:

1. How difficult or how easy does one write each test item in terms of complexity?
2. What subject matter is to be covered on the test?
3. Which is the most appropriate way for pupils to reveal what has been learned? Different ways of revealing

learning may include paper/pencil tests such as is used in the NAEP tests; however, there are numerous additional ways such as experiments, demonstrations, hands on approaches, and art work, among others.

4. How much emphasis should be placed upon subject matter content in the tests as compared to skills and attitudes?

5. What meanings are to be given to test results of pupils?

If, for example, forty per cent of nine year olds cannot write a meaningful sentence, according to NAEP results, then the teacher needs to assist pupils in writing meaningful sentences. It is difficult to know what is meant by a meaningful sentence, according to NAEP workers and measurement specialists.

Constructivism has the most merit of all approaches in ascertaining what pupils have learned. Why? The evaluation is not a one shot approach, but can be ongoing and continuous. Within a learning situation then, the teacher appraises how well a pupil is doing. The results may be obtained from teacher observation as well as test results. Feedback is then given to the pupil on what can be done to achieve sequentially (Ediger, 1996).

Perhaps, all of the approaches mentioned above have some merit. However, the goal is to assist pupils to achieve more optimally, not to obtain test scores for comparisons to be made among pupils nor to minimize human values of individual learners. If pupils fail, teachers need to have information on guiding pupils individually to be successful learners.

REFERENCES

Alrasian, Peter W., and Mary E. Walsh (1997), "Cautions for Classroom Constructivists," *Education Digest*, Vol. 62, No. 8, page 63, (Condensed from *Phi Delta Kappa*, Vol. 78, No. 2, Pages 444-449.

Clinton, Bill (1997), "President Clinton's Call for Action," *Education Digest*, Vol. 62, No. 8, Pages 4-7.

Ediger, Marlow (1977), "Slogans in Education and in Society, *Journal of Instructional Psychology*, Vol. 24, No. 1, Pages 37-41.

Ediger, Marlow (1996). *Essays in School Administration*, Kirksville, Missouri: Simpson Publishing, Pages 93 and 94.

Kakkar, S.B. (1997), Crisis in Education in India, *The Educational Review*, Vol. 102, No. 1 Pages 1 and 2.

Illich, Ivan (1972). *De-Schooling Society*. New York: Harper and Row.

Additional Reading

Bhaskara Rao, Digumarti (1994). *Scientific Aptitude*. New Delhi: Ashish Publishing House. ISBN 81-7024-658-X.

Bhaskara Rao, Digumarti (1995). *Animal Kingdom*. New Delhi: Discovery Publishing House. ISBN 81-7141-274-2.

Bhaskara Rao, Digumarti (1995). *Batracology*. New Delhi: Discovery Publishing House. ISBN 81-7141-279-3.

Bhaskara Rao, Digumarti (1996). *Scientific Attitude vis-a-vis Scientific Aptitude*. New Delhi: Discovery Publishing House. ISBN 81-7141-308-0.

Bhaskara Rao, Digumarti, ed. (1996). *Encyclopaedia of Education For All*. 5 Vols. New Delhi: APH Publishing Corporation. ISBN 81-7024-759-4 (set).

Vol. I Education For All: The World Conference. ISBN 81-7024-760-8.

Vol. II Education For All: The EPA-9 Summit. ISBN 81-7024-761-6.

Vol. III Education For All: Quality Education For All. ISBN 81-7024-762-4.

Vol. IV Education For All: Planning and Monitoring. ISBN 81-7024-763-2.

Vol. V Education For All: The Indian Scenario. 81-7024-764-0.

Bhaskara Rao, Digumarti, ed. (1996). *Global Perceptions on Peace Education*, 3 Vo!s. New Delhi: Discovery Publishing House. ISBN 81-7141-319-6.

Bhaskara Rao, Digumarti, ed. (1996). *National Policy on Education*, 2 Vols. New Delhi: Anmol Publications Pvt. Ltd. ISBN 81-7488-323-1.

Bhaskara Rao, Digumarti, ed. (1997). *Care the Child*, 2 Vols. New Delhi: Discovery Publishing House. ISBN 81-7141-394-3.

Bhaskara Rao, Digumarti, ed. (1997). *Education for the 21st Century*. New Delhi: Discovery Publishing House. ISBN 81-7141-389-7.

Bhaskara Rao, Digumarti, ed. (1997). *Reflections on Scientific Attitude*. New Delhi: Discovery Publishing House. ISBN 81-7141-328-5.

Bhaskara Rao, Digumarti (1997). *Scientific Attitude*. New Delhi: Discovery Publishing House. ISBN 81-7141-381-1.

Bhaskara Rao, Digumarti, ed. (1997). *Success Story of a Primary Education Project*. New Delhi: APH Publishing Corporation. ISBN 81-7024-850-7.

Bhaskara Rao, Digumarti, ed. (1997). *World Food Summit*. New Delhi: Discovery Publishing House. ISBN 81-7141-386-2.

Bhaskara Rao, Digumarti, ed. (1998). *Adolescence Education*. New Delhi: Discovery Publishing House. ISBN 81-7141-432-X.

Bhaskara Rao, Digumarti, ed. (1998). *Community and School Nutrition Education*. New Delhi: Discovery Publishing House. ISBN 81-7141-435-4.

Bhaskara Rao, Digumarti, ed. (1998). *District Primary Education Programme*. New Delhi: Discovery Publishing House. ISBN 81-7141-396-X.

Bhaskara Rao, Digumarti, ed. (1998). *Earth Summit*, 2 Vols. New Delhi: Discovery Publishing House. ISBN 81-7141-435-4.

Bhaskara Rao, Digumarti, ed. (1998). *National Policy on Education: Towards an Enlightened and Humane Society*. New Delhi: Discovery Publishing House. ISBN 81-7141-426-5.

Bhaskara Rao, Digumarti, ed. (1998). *Reforming School Education*. New Delhi: Discovery Publishing House. ISBN 81-7141-403-6.

Bhaskara Rao, Digumarti, ed. (1998). *Teacher Education in India*. New Delhi: Discovery Publishing House. ISBN 81-7141-406-0.

Bhaskara Rao, Digumarti, ed. (1998). *World Summit for Social Development*. New Delhi: Discovery Publishing House. ISBN 81-7141-420-6.

Bhaskara Rao, Digumarti, ed. (2000). *Education For All: Achieving the Goal*. 3 Vols. New Delhi: APH Publishing Corporation. ISBN 81-7648-152-1.

Vol. I The Global Consensus. ISBN 81-7648-153-X.

Vol. II Mid-Decade Review Reports of Regional Seminars. ISBN 81-7648-154-8.

Vol. III Issues and Trends. ISBN 81-7648-155-6.

Bhaskara Rao, Digumarti, ed. (2000). *International Encyclopaedia of AIDS*, 11 Vols. in 13 Parts. New Delhi: Discovery Publishing House. ISBN 81-7141-465-6 (set).

Vol. 1 Introduction to HIV/AIDS. ISBN 81-7141-523-7.

Vol. 2 HIV/AIDS—Issues and Challenges, 2 Parts. ISBN 81-7141-524-5.

Vol. 3 HIV/AIDS—Socio Economic Realities. ISBN 81-7141-525-3.

Vol. 4 HIV/AIDS Law Ethics and Human Rights, 2 Parts. ISBN 81-7141-526-1

Vol. 5 AIDS and NGOs. ISBN 81-7141-527-X.

Vol. 6 AIDS and Home Care. ISBN 81-7141-528-8.

Vol. 7 STD Case Management. ISBN 81-7141-529-6.

Vol. 8 HIV Prevention and Care—Teaching Modules for Nurses and Midwives. ISBN 81-7141-530-X.

Vol. 9 HIV/AIDS Prevention Education for Educational Institutions. ISBN 81-7141-531-8.

Vol.10 Instructional Modules for AIDS Education. ISBN 81-7141-532-6.

Vol.11 School Health Education to Prevent AIDS and STD—A Package for Curriculum Planners. ISBN 81-7141-533-4.

Bhaskara Rao, Digumarti, ed. (2000). *International Encyclopaedia of Science and Technology Education*. 11 Volumes. New Delhi: Discovery Publishing House. ISBN 81-7141-548-2 (set).

Vol. 1 Science and Technology Education. ISBN 81-7141-568-7.

Vol. 2 Science Education in Developing Countries. ISBN 81-7141-570-9.

Vol. 3 Organisational Structure of Science. ISBN 81-7141-570-9.

Vol. 4 Science Education in Asia and the Pacific. ISBN 81-7141-571-7.

Vol. 5 Science and Technology Education for All. ISBN 81-7141-572-5.

Vol. 6 Values, Ethics, Talent and Girls in Science and Technology Education. ISBN 81-7141-573-3.

Vol. 7 Popularization of Science and Technology Education. ISBN 81-7141-574-1.

Vol. 8 Science, Power and Society. ISBN 81-7141-575-X.

Vol. 9 Information Technology. ISBN 81-7141-576-8.

Vol.10 Teacher Training in Science and Technology Education. ISBN 81-7141-577-6.

Vol.11 Science, Technology and Society: A Curriculum Framework. ISBN 81-7141-578-4.

Bhaskara Rao, Digumarti, ed. (2001). *Distance Education in Different Countries*. New Delhi: APH Publishing Corporation. ISBN 81-7648-229-3.

Bhaskara Rao, Digumarti, ed. (2001). *Decentralised Management of Education (Management of Education in Panchayati Raj and Municipal Bodies)*. New Delhi: Discovery Publishing House. ISBN 81-7141-617-9.

Bhaskara Rao, Digumarti, ed. (2001). *Electrochemistry for Environmental Protection*. New Delhi: Discovery Publishing House. ISBN 81-7141-619-5.

Bhaskara Rao, Digumarti, ed. (2001). *Global Educational Studies*. New Delhi: Discovery Publishing House. ISBN 81-7141-616-0.

Bhaskara Rao, Digumarti, ed. (2001). *Global Synthesis of Educational Assessment*. New Delhi: Discovery Publishing House. ISBN 81-7141-613-6.

Bhaskara Rao, Digumarti, ed. (2001). *International Encyclopaedia of Human Rights*, 7 Volumes in 13 Parts. New Delhi: Discovery Publishing House. ISBN 81-7141-567-9 (set).

Vol. 1 International Instruments of Human Rights, 2 Parts. ISBN 81-7141-595-4.

Vol. 2 Regional Instruments of Human Rights. ISBN 81-7141-604-7.

Vol. 3 Human Rights and The United Nations, 2 Parts. ISBN 81-7141-605-5.

Vol. 4 Fact Files of Human Rights, 2 Parts. ISBN 81-7141-606-3.

Vol. 5 Study Stories of Human Rights, 3 Parts.
ISBN 81-7141-607-1.

Vol. 6 International Meetings on Human Rights, 2 Parts.
ISBN 81-7141-608-X.

Vol. 7 Professional Training in Human Rights.
ISBN 81-7141-609-8.

Bhaskara Rao, Digumarti, ed. (2001). *Jomtein Decade of Education*. New Delhi: Discovery Publishing House. ISBN 81-7141-618-7.

Bhaskara Rao, Digumarti, ed. (2001). *Nuclear Materials: Issues and Concerns*, 2 Vols. New Delhi: Discovery Publishing House. ISBN 81-7141-611-X.

Bhaskara Rao, Digumarti, ed. (2001). *World Conference on Education for All*. New Delhi: APH Publishing Corporation. ISBN 81-7648-274-9.

Bhaskara Rao, Digumarti, ed. (2001). *World Conference on Higher Education*. New Delhi: Discovery Publishing House. ISBN 81-7141-610-1.

Bhaskara Rao, Digumarti, ed. (2001). *World Conference on Science*. New Delhi: Discovery Publishing House. ISBN 81-7141-612-8.

Bhaskara Rao, Digumarti, ed. (2002). *Inspiring Experiences in Teacher Education*. New Delhi: Discovery Publishing House.

Bhaskara Rao, Digumarti, ed. (2002). *International Studies in Education*. New Delhi: Discovery Publishing House.

Bhaskara Rao, Digumarti, ed. (2002). *Military Conversion: Impact on Science and Technology*. New Delhi: Discovery Publishing House. ISBN 81-7141-643-8.

Bhaskara Rao, Digumarti, ed. (2002). *United Nations Millennium Summit*. New Delhi: Discovery Publishing House. ISBN 81-7141-632-2.

Bhaskara Rao, Digumarti, ed, (2002). *World Assembly on Ageing*. New Delhi: Discovery Publishing House. ISBN 81-7141-637-3.

Bhaskara Rao, Digumarti, ed. (2002). *World Conference on Human Rights*. New Delhi: Discovery Publishing House.

Bhaskara Rao, Digumarti, ed. (2003). *World Education Forum*. New Delhi: Discovery Publishing House.

Bhaskara Rao, Digumarti, ed. (2003). *Education Employment and Human Resource Development*. New Delhi: Discovery Publishing House.

Bhaskara Rao, Digumarti, ed. (2003). *European Education and Teachers*. New Delhi: Discovery Publishing House.

Bhaskara Rao, Digumarti, ed. (2003). *Teachers in a Changing World*. New Delhi: Discovery Publishing House.

Bhaskara Rao, Digumarti, ed. (2003). *Successful Schooling*. New Delhi: Discovery Publishing House.

Bhaskara Rao, Digumarti, ed. (2003). *Learning To Live Together*. New Delhi: Discovery Publishing House.

Bhaskara Rao, Digumarti, C.A.P. Swamy and B.S.V. Dutt (1997). *Self Evaluation in Student Teaching*. New Delhi: Discovery Publishing House. ISBN 81-7141-374-9.

Bhaskara Rao, Digumarti, C. Sridevi and K. Vijaya (1995). *Achievement in Social Studies*. New Delhi: Discovery Publishing House. ISBN 81-7141-281-5.

Bhaskara Rao, Digumarti and Digumarti Pushpa Latha (1994). *Achievement in Biology*. New Delhi: Discovery Publishing House. ISBN 81-7141-264-5.

Bhaskara Rao, Digumarti and Digumarti Pushpa Latha (1995). *Achievement in English*. New Delhi: Discovery Publishing House. ISBN 81-7141-283-1.

Bhaskara Rao, Digumarti and Digumarti Pushpa Latha (1995). *Achievement in Science*. New Delhi: Discovery Publishing House. ISBN 81-7141-280-7.

Bhaskara Rao, Digumarti and Digumarti Pushpa Latha (1995). *Achievement in Mathematics*. New Delhi: Discovery Publishing House. ISBN 81-7141-278-5.

Bhaskara Rao, Digumarti and Digumarti Pushpa Latha, eds. (1998). *International Encyclopaedia of Women*, 5 Vols. New Delhi: Discovery Publishing House. ISBN 81-7141-410-9.

Vol. 1 Status of World's Women. ISBN 81-7141-494-X.

Vol. 2 Women, Education and Empowerment. ISBN 81-7141-498-2.

Vol. 3 Women Challenges and Advancement. ISBN 81-7141-497-4.

Vol. 4 Women and Family Health. ISBN 81-7141-497-4.

Vol. 5 Women and International Action. ISBN 81-7141-498-2.

Bhaskara Rao, Digumarti, Digumarti Pushpa Latha and Digumarti Harshitha, eds. (2001). *Biological Warfcre*. New Delhi: Discovery Publishing House. ISBN 81-7141-597-0.

Bhaskara Rao, Digumarti, Digumarti Pushpa Latha and Digumarti Harshitha, eds. (2001). *Women as Educators*. New Delhi: Discovery Publishing House. ISBN 81-7141-602-0.

Bhaskara Rao, Digumarti and Digumarti Harshitha (2001). *Education in India*. New Delhi: APH Publishing Corporation. ISBN 81-7648-207-2.

Bhaskara Rao, Digumarti, and Digumarti Harshitha eds. (2001). *Assessing Learning Achievement*. New Delhi: Discovery Publishing House. ISBN 81-7141-601-2.

Bhaskara Rao, Digumarti and Digumarti Harshitha, eds. (2001). *Energy Security*. New Delhi: Discovery Publishing House. ISBN 81-7141-598-9.

Bhaskara Rao, Digumarti, D. Harshitha and K.R.S.S. Rao, eds. (1999). *Advanced Biotechnology*. New Delhi: Discovery Publishing House. ISBN 81-7141-516-4.

Bhaskara Rao, Digumarti and D. Sridhar (2002). *Job Satisfaction of School Teachers*. New Delhi: Discovery Publishing House.

Bhaskara Rao, Digumarti and K.R.S. Sambasiva Rao, eds. (1996). *Current Trends in Indian Education*. New Delhi: Discovery Publishing House. ISBN 81-7141-311-0.

Bhaskara Rao, Digumarti and K. Vijaya (1995). *A Text Book Evaluation*. Ambala Cantt: The Associated Publishers.

Bhaskara Rao, Digumarti and N.V.M. Mohana Rao (2002). *Problems of Mentally Handicapped*. New Delhi: Discovery Publishing House.

Bhaskara Rao, Digumarti, V.V. Rao, V.V. Lakshmi and V.V. Krishna, eds. (2000). *Status and Advancement of Women*. New Delhi: APH Publishing Corporation. ISBN 81-7648-169-6.

Babu, P.C. and Digumarti Bhaskara Rao, ed. (2004). *Flowers of Wisdom*. New Delhi: Discovery Publishing House.

Bhagya Lakshmi, Lingineni and Digumarti Bhaskara Rao, ed. (2000). *Reading and Comprehension*. New Delhi: Discovery Publishing House. ISBN 81-7141-543-1.

Bhuvaneswara Lakshmi, G. and Digumarti Bhaskara Rao, ed. (2000). *Attitude Towards Science*. New Delhi: Discovery Publishing House. ISBN 81-7141-541-6.

Devraj, T.A.S. & Digumarti Bhaskara Rao, ed. (1997). *Trace Analysis of Uranium and Thorum*. New Delhi: Discovery Publishing House. ISBN 81-7141-375-7.

Durga Rani, K. & Digumarti Bhaskara Rao, ed. (2000). *Educational Aspirations and Scientific Attitudes*. New Delhi: Discovery Publishing House. ISBN 81-7141-555-55.

Dutt, B.S.V. & Digumarti Bhaskara Rao (2001). *Empowering Primary Teachers*. New Delhi: Discovery Publishing House. ISBN 81-7141-615-2.

Ediger, Marlow & Digumarti Bhaskara Rao (1996). *Science Curriculum,* New Delhi: Discovery Publishing House. ISBN 81-7141-321-8.

Ediger, Marlow & Digumarti Bhaskara Rao (2000). *Teaching Mathematics Successfully*. New Delhi: Discovery Publishing House. ISBN 81-7141-552-0.

Ediger, Marlow & Digumarti Bhaskara Rao (2000). *Teaching Reading Successfully*. New Delhi: Discovery Publishing House ISBN 81-7141-556-3.

Ediger Marlow & Digumarti Bhaskara Rao (2001). *Teaching Science Successfully*. New Delhi: Discovery Publishing House. ISBN 81-7141-600-4.

Ediger, Marlow & Digumarti Bhaskara Rao (2001). *Teaching Social Studies Successfully*. New Delhi: Discovery Publishing House. ISBN 81-7141-596-2.

Ediger, Marlow & Digumarti Bhaskara Rao (2003). *Philosophy and Curriculum*. New Delhi: Discovery Publishing House. ISBN 81-7141-631-4.

Ediger, Marlow and Digumarti Bhaskara Rao (2003). *Improving School Administration*. New Delhi: Discovery Publishing House: ISBN 81-7141-633-0.

Ediger, Marlow and Digumarti Bhaskara Rao (2003). *Elementary Curriculum*. New Delhi: Discovery Publishing House.

Ediger, Marlow and Digumarti Bhaskara Rao (2003). *Language Arts Curriculum*. New Delhi Discovery Publishing House.

Ediger, Marlow and Digumarti Bhaskara Rao (2003). *Teaching Language Arts Successfully*. New Delhi: Discovery Publishing House.

Ediger, Marlow and Digumarti Bhaskara Rao (2003). *Teaching Mathematics in Elementary Schools*. New Delhi: Discovery Publishing House.

Ediger, Marlow and Digumarti Bhaskara Rao, (2003). *Teaching Social Studies in Elementary School*. New Delhi: Discovery Publishing House.

Jayasree, Kandi and Digumarti Bhaskara Rao, ed. (1999). *Correlates of Socialisation*. New Delhi: Discovery Publishing House. ISBN 81-7141-517-2.

John Babu, Ch., T.J.R. Prasad, G.M. Madhukar and Digumarti Bhaskara Rao, eds. (2001). *Problem Solving in Mathematics*. New Delhi: APH Publishing Corporation. ISBN 81-7648-273-0.

Jyothi, Nirmala and Digumarti Bhaskara Rao, ed (2002). *Non-detention System in Education*. New Delhi: Discovery Publishing House.

Marja, Talvi and Digumarti Bhaskara Rao, eds. (1996). *Educational Leadership and Social Changes*. New Delhi: Discovery Publishing House. ISBN 81-7141-320-X.

Prabhakaram, K.S. and Digumarti Bhaskara Rao, ed. (1998). *Concept Attainment Model in Mathematics Teaching*. New Delhi: Discovery Publishing. ISBN 81-7141-424-9.

Prasanth Kumar, J, and Digumarti Bhaskara Rao, ed. (1998). *Effectiveness of Distance Education System*. New Delhi: Discovery Publishing House. ISBN 81-7141-437-0.

Prasanth Kumar, J. and Digumarti Bhaksara Rao and G. Sundara Rao, eds. (2000). *Open University Student Support Services*. New Delhi: Discovery Publishing House: ISBN 81-7141-550-4.

Ramatulasamma K. and Digumarti Bhaskara Rao, ed. (2002). *Job Satisfaction of Teacher Educators*. New Delhi: Discovery Publishing House.

Rama Krishnaiah, D. and Digumarti Bhaskara Rao, ed. (1998). *Job Satisfaction of College Teachers*. New Delhi: Discovery Publishing House: ISBN 81-7141-438-9.

Ramakumar, Ratnam and Digumarti Bhaskara Rao, ed. (2003). *Dukkha: Suffering in Early Buddhism*. New Delhi: Discovery Publishing House.

Ramesh, Ganta and Digumarti Bhaskara Rao, eds. (1998). *Environmental Education: Problems and Prospects*. New Delhi: Discovery Publishing House. ISBN 81-7141-423-0.

Rathaiah, L. and Digumarti Bhaskara Rao, eds. (1997). *International Innovations in Education*. New Delhi: Discovery Publishing House. ISBN 81-7141-359-5.

Rathaiah, Lavu, Digumarti Bhaskara Rao and Paturi Koteswara Rao. (1997). *Achievement Correlates*. New Delhi: Discovery Publishing House. ISBN 81-7141-385-4.

Reddy, Sudhakar and Digumarti Bhaskara Rao, ed. (2002). *Creativity in Adolescents*. New Delhi: Discovery Publishing House.

Reddy, M.S. and Digumarti Bhaskara Rao, ed. (2003). *Creativity in College Students*, New Delhi: Discovery Publishing House.

Sanjeeva Rao, P.C. and Digumarti Bhaskara Rao, ed. (1996). *A Text Book of Geology*. New Delhi: Discovery Publishing House. ISBN 81-7141-313-7.

Satya Narayana, V. and Digumarti Bhaskara Rao, ed. (2001). *Physical Education, Social Attitudes and Leadership Qualities*. New Delhi: ISBN 81-7141-593-8.

Srinivasulu Reddy, M., K.R.S. Sambasiva Rao and Digumarti Bhaskara Rao, ed. (1999). *A Text Book of Aquaculture*. New Delhi: Discovery Publishing House. ISBN 81-7141-482-6.

Vanaja, M. and Digumarti Bhaskara Rao, ed. (1999). *Inquiry Training Model*. New Delhi: Discovery Publishing House. ISBN 81-7141-515-6.

Valeri V. Koustiouk and Digumarti Bhaskara Rao, ed. (2002). *A Text Book of Cryogenics*. New Delhi: Discovery Publishing House. ISBN 80-7141-642-X.

Valeri V. Koustiouk and Digumarti Bhaskara Rao, ed. (2002). *Refrigeration and Environment*. New Delhi: Discovery Publishing House.

Veena Kumari, Balusu and Digumarti Bhaskara Rao (1996). *Operation Black Board*. New Delhi: APH Publishing Corporation. ISBN 81-7024-711-X.

Veena Kumari, B. and Digumarti Bhaskara Rao, ed. (2000). *Psycho-Social Correlates of Achievement*. New Delhi: Discovery Publishing House. ISBN 81-7141-547-4.

Venkata Rao, P. and Digumarti Bhaskara Rao (1989). *A Text Book of Zoology—Junior Intermediate*. Guntur: Vignan Publishers.

Venkata Rao, P. and Digumarti Bhaskara Rao (1989). *A Text Book of Zoology—Senior Intermediate*. Guntur: Vignan Publishers.

Venugopala Rao, K. and Digumarti Bhaskara Rao, ed. (2000). *Teacher Morale in Secondary Schools*. New Delhi: Discovery Publishing House. ISBN 81-7141-551-2.

Vidya, C. and Digumarti Bhaskara Rao, ed. (1996). *A Text Book of Nutrition*. New Delhi: Discovery Publishing House. ISBN 81-7141-309-9.

Vijaya Bharathi, D. and Digumarti Bhaskara Rao, ed. (2000). *Educational Philosophies of Swami Vivekanand and John Dewey*. New Delhi: APH Publishing Corporation. ISBN 81-7648-202-1.

Bhaskara Rao, Digumarti. (1996). *Dhrushya Sravana Bodhanapakaranamulu* (Audio Visual Teaching Aids). Guntur: Nagarjuna Publishers.

Bhaskara Rao, Digumarti (1993). *Jeevasashtra Bodhana* (Teaching of Biology. Guntur: Nagarjuna Publishers.

Bhaskara Rao, Digumarti (1995). *Vignanasasthra Bodhana*. (Teaching of Science). Guntur: Nagarjuna Publishers.

Bhaskara Rao, Digumarti (1997). *Vidya Manovignana Sashtram*. (Educational Psychology). Guntur: Creative Press.

Bhaskara Rao, Digumarti (1998). *DSC Study Material*. Guntur: Nagarjuna Publishers.

Bhaskara Rao, Digumarti (1998). *Upadhyayudu Vidya* (Teacher and Education). Guntur: Nagarjuna Publishers.

Bhaskara Rao, Digumarti (1998). *Vidya Dhrukpadhalu*. (Perspectives of Education). Guntur: Nagarjuna Publishers.

Bhaskara Rao, Digumarti (1999). *EdCET Teaching Aptitude*. Guntur: Nagarjuna Publishers.

Bhaskara Rao, Digumarti (2001). *Bharata Samajamulo Upadhayayudu Vidya* (Teacher and Education in Emerging Indian Society). Guntur: Nagarjuna Publishers.

Bhaskara Rao, Digumarti (2001). *Bhoutika Sastra Bodhana Padhatulu* (Methods of Teaching Physical Science). Guntur: Nagarjuna Publishers.

Bhaskara Rao, Digumarti (2001). *Jeeva Sastra Bodhana Padhatulu* (Methods of Teaching Biological Science). Guntur: Nagarjuna Publishers.

Bhaskara Rao, Digumarti (2001). *Vidya Manovignana Sastram* (Educational Psychology). Guntur: Nagarjuna Publishers.

Bhaskara Rao, Digumarti (2003). *Vidya Sanketika Sastram* (Educational Technology). Guntur: Nagarjuna Publishers.

Bhaskara Rao, Digumarti (2003). *Pathasala Paripalana Nirvahana* (School Administration and Management). Guntur: Nagarjuna Publishers.

Index

Index